Member Management Essentials for Chambers of Commerce

Scott C. Stevenson, Editor

WILEY

978-1-118-69048-2   ISBN

978-1-118-70387-8   ISBN (online)

Membership Management Essentials For Chambers of Commerce

Published by

Stevenson, Inc.

P.O. Box 4528 • Sioux City, Iowa • 51104
Phone 712.239.3010 • Fax 712.239.2166
www.stevensoninc.com

Membership Management Essentials for Chambers of Commerce

READY, SET, GO: PLAN FOR SUCCESS

Those chambers of commerce that are growing and achieving are those that have a thoroughly-documented plan, a yearlong plan sometimes referred to as an operational plan. That plan is the result of a planning process which begins with evaluating historical data and then involving key people — board members, community leaders, staff and others — in a planning process to establish yearly goals and action plans. This process should also include an honest evaluation of your chamber's strengths and weaknesses. A thorough review of past results will help create an operational plan that's challenging but realistic.

Operational Plans Have Seven Essential Elements

The most successful Chambers of Commerce have a yearlong operational plan in place. Staff, board members and key community leaders should be involved in creating or shaping the operational plan.

The seven essential elements of an annual operational plan include:

1. Evaluation of current and historical data: membership growth/decline, retention rates, dues structure, member benefits, key achievements, internal and external challenges and more.

2. Establishing key goals for the upcoming year (e.g., new members, retention, programming achievements, changes to dues structure/procedure and more).

3. Setting quantifiable objectives that support those goals.

4. Designing action plans that spell out how those objectives will be met (e.g., membership campaign strategies, retention strategies and more).

5. Creating a detailed yearlong calendar that identifies everything that will occur by when and who is responsible.

6. Monitoring the plan's progress throughout the year and making adjustments as needed.

7. Evaluating the plan at year-end in light of what was achieved or what fell short of expectations.

Start by Evaluating Historical Data

As you work to prepare an operational plan for the upcoming year — a plan that identifies goals, objectives, strategies, action plans and timetables — it's critical that you begin by evaluating what is currently being done and making changes based on the success (or lack of) of existing programs.

As a first step in the planning process, it will be enormously helpful if you can evaluate the current year in light of past years' results. Examples of historical review may include:

- Membership growth/decline.
- Member retention/attrition rates.
- Dues structure.
- Member renewal procedures.
- Membership categories and accompanying benefits.
- Volunteer involvement.

As you evaluate the existing year's programs in light of previous years' results, when possible, attempt to quantify each program in terms of: net revenue, the cost-to-revenue ratio, the percentage of staff time and budget required to carry out the program and a comparison to other programs.

In addition, weigh each program in light of its long- versus short-term payoff.

Examples of individual aspects to be evaluated include:

- Mission.
- Existing by-laws.
- Member recruitment efforts.
- Member renewal efforts.
- Economic development efforts — attracting new business, industrial park, supporting existing businesses, etc.
- Fundraising efforts — golf classic, gala, etc.
- Ambassador program.
- After-hours program.
- Ribbon-cutting events.
- Legislative/lobbying efforts.
- Sponsored events.

These program evaluation results will serve as your planning foundation.

Membership Management Essentials for Chambers of Commerce

Planning Procedures: Setting Membership Goals

The science of setting membership goals is as much about analyzing internal strengths and weaknesses as it is about reviewing external factors. For the leadership team at the Greater Oklahoma City Chamber (Oklahoma City, OK) the planning process starts with an honest assessment of where the organization is, compared to where they want it to be. Vice President of Membership Lisa Boevers explains their approach:

"When we claim to represent the business industry, we want to speak truthfully. A wide spectrum of companies make up the business community in Oklahoma City, and our membership should reflect that diversity. Therefore, when setting goals we first look at the composition of our member categories. This involves identifying the number of members we have in each category and comparing that to the entire business sector. This reveals both areas of strength as well as gaps we need to fill to better represent the industry. It is important to build on strengths and pursue more members in those categories. With gaps, they often happen simply because a certain type of member wasn't asked to join. This demonstrates why analyzing internal strengths and weaknesses is so important. Sometimes members haven't joined because they weren't asked."

Second, the chamber determines where it is making an impact and who benefits from its activities. The OKC Chamber focuses on advocacy and policy, community development, education and workforce issues, and also functions as the local convention and visitors bureau. "These areas of focus make it easier to identify who benefits most from the chamber, and makes it clear to whom membership is most attractive, guiding our outreach strategy and goals," says Boevers.

Finally, in the planning process the chamber determines how to best use volunteers. According to Boevers, "It is important to have volunteers who represent the diversity of the business sector in order to attract a wide range of members. We make it easy for volunteers to recruit by encouraging them to speak about the chamber to the companies they work with or would like to work with on a daily basis."

To summarize, the science of setting membership goals involves analysis of strengths and weaknesses, current composition of member categories, identifying areas of impact and who benefits most, and volunteer involvement. It is also helpful to look at the marketplace and capitalize on trends impacting the industry. This allows an organization to shape its messaging to have the greatest effect. Considering these elements as you plan for the future will position your organization for success.

Source: Lisa Boevers, Vice President of Membership, Greater Oklahoma City Chamber of Commerce, Oklahoma City, OK. E-mail: lboevers@okcchamber.com

Tailor Chamber Dues to Member Industries

Membership dues structures that address individual member needs send a powerful message of welcoming.

"Having dues that reflect someone's industry realities, instead of just lumping them in with a lot of businesses very different from their own, makes people feel like you know their business and are there to work for them," says Colleen Burke, director of member services, Park City Chamber of Commerce Convention & Visitors Bureau (Park City, UT).

As an outdoor tourism hot spot, Park City has an economy dominated by lodging, transportation and booking, Burke says, and chamber dues reflect the realities of those industries. Dues for booking services, for example, are based on the number of agents a firm employs. Dues for hotels, restaurants and transportation providers are similarly tied to the number of rooms, square feet, and vehicles a business manages. Banks pay one flat fee — an acknowledgment of the reality that Park City has only resort branches and no large headquarter institutions, says Burke.

While the dues structure is intricate, Burke says she is not concerned about overcomplication. "There's really no harm in adding new membership categories as new industries grow and evolve in your area. People look to their category and understand that this is just a way to make sure everyone is getting the benefits they paid for. It's a way to be fair to everyone."

View the membership dues structure online at: http://www.parkcityinfo.com/static/index.cfm?contentID=835.

Source: Colleen Burke, Director of Member Services, Park City Chamber of Commerce Convention & Visitors Bureau, Park City, UT. E-mail: colleen@parkcityinfo.com

Ignite Creative Thinking With Staff/Board Retreat

A retreat for staff and/or board members can foster creative thinking while providing an inspiring, focused environment in which to brainstorm and collaborate.

Members of the Pike County Chamber of Commerce (Milford, PA) are reaping the benefits of past retreat for its board of directors, says Scott J. Weiland, executive director (see list of newly implemented ideas, right).

Through a retreat, Weiland says, "valuable information can be derived and a shared vision for the future of your organization can be formed." He emphasizes that making the most of a retreat requires stakeholder support of the process and use of information garnered to shape the future of the organization.

Three Months of Planning Leads Up to One-day Retreat

The chamber's business/education committee organized the one-day retreat with the help of Joseph Blanco, organizational development consultant (Shohola, PA). Planning began three months prior to the event. The committee developed the agenda and program, with Blanco joining the group on a regular basis at meetings and by e-mail to help design an effective program.

The retreat, attended by 18 of the 25 board members, cost approximately $1,000 for consultant fees, facility rental and materials. Members unable to attend e-mailed ideas ahead of time to be included in discussions and brainstorming sessions. Tools that helped make the retreat productive included a laptop, projector, flip-chart pads and easels, music, a 10-minute training video on the creative problem-solving process, handouts and the agenda.

At the retreat, Weiland says, "warm-up questions included interaction between groups of four where we told a brief personal success milestone to each other and rotated to different tables to repeat them, so all participants were able to connect." Additional team-building/problem-solving exercises included briefly working in teams of four to brainstorm and offer solutions to problem scenarios.

Blanco says the exercises also helped participants learn the skills needed to be creative during the retreat.

Post-retreat Report Helps Prioritize Next Steps to Success

A detailed four-page report created post-retreat included all brainstorming ideas and a breakdown of issues discussed, categorized as either "Continue," "Start" or "Stop." The categories detailed which programs/issues need to be started, which ongoing issues should be continued and which should be stopped. The report was accompanied by an e-mail overview of the retreat and sent to all directors, including those who could not attend.

Weiland said they would revisit the report in the fall to see how to build their programs and review what they have accomplished since the retreat.

Sources: Scott J. Weiland, Executive Director, The Pike County Chamber of Commerce, Milford, PA.
Joseph Blanco, Organizational Development Consultant, Shohola, PA.
E-mail: j@jblanco.us

Retreat Sparks Fresh Ideas

A retreat for board members of the Pike County Chamber of Commerce (Milford, PA) energized the chamber with fresh ideas to better serve members.

Retreat-generated ideas the chamber is implementing include:

- **Sharpening marketing plan:** The Internet marketing committee developed a marketing plan for the chamber and is developing efforts to promote the chamber in the county and beyond, efforts not clearly defined before the retreat.

- **Boosting meeting productivity:** Each committee has been asked to be more productive when conducting meetings, including writing an agenda and taking meeting minutes.

- **Pumping up communication:** The chamber has increased electronic communication, launching a new e-mail newsletter, which is already generating positive member feedback.

- **Creating a member benefit survey:** The business/education committee drafted a survey to strengthen or identify key membership benefits, including networking, healthcare, communications and seminars/training.

Tap Your Organization's Mission to Build a Mission Acronym

The Wayne County Area Chamber of Commerce (Richmond, IN) is known as the Chamber P.L.U.S., with P.L.U.S. standing for Promote, Lead, Unite and Serve.

Chamber officials created the acronym by pulling key words from its mission, says Suzanne Derengowski, interim CEO.

Consider pulling the key words from your mission statement to create an acronym that will benefit your members and community in the following ways:

- Creating an easily identifiable way for members to remember the mission and convey that to nonmembers.
- Emphasizing key points of your mission, creating focus and guidance for members.
- Offering a new way for members and the community to identify your program and connect with your purpose.

Source: Suzanne Derengowski, Interim CEO, Wayne County Area Chamber of Commerce, Richmond, IN. E-mail: suzanne@wcareachamber.org

Educating the Public: Be Prepared to Say What You Are Not

Steve Hatcher, President/CEO of the Oswego Chamber of Commerce (Oswego, IL) says clarifying what your organization is not helps members, would-be members, and the public identify the benefits of joining the organization.

One of the most common misconceptions about a chamber is that it is a part of government and supported by tax dollars. "While chambers often advocate the business point of view at the local, state and even national level, we have absolutely no jurisdiction in making and enforcing regulations," says Hatcher. For example, Hatcher says you shouldn't call the chamber if a stoplight isn't working or if the neighbor's grass is too high.

Another misconception is that a chamber is the same as a Better Business Bureau (BBB). "While chambers represent the interests of business, the BBB represents the interests of the public," says Hatcher, "But rest assured we'll be happy to refer a member business for any products or services needed. We'll also tell you if a business is a member or not, and if we've received any complaints."

Hatcher says it's important to try to provide people with answers to their questions, even if it doesn't involve your organization's responsibilities. "I don't want to be in a position to make people angry," says Hatcher, so he still makes courtesy calls to the local government to refer a caller to the right contact or get the appropriate information.

A third misconception deals with the relationship between the local chamber, state chamber and the United States Chamber. Local chambers may choose to become a member of a state or national organization, says Hatcher, just as a local business may choose to become a member of the local chamber. "Voluntary membership is the key," he says. In Hatcher's case, the Oswego Chamber of Commerce is a member of both the Illinois State Chamber and the United States Chamber. "But it's an endless process to educate people," says Hatcher.

Source: Steve Hatcher, President/CEO, Oswego Chamber of Commerce, Oswego, IL. Email: steve@oswegochamber.org

Membership Management Essentials for Chambers of Commerce

IDENTIFY AND STRENGTHEN MEMBER BENEFITS

Your ability to attract new members and retain existing ones is a function of what businesses perceive as direct and indirect benefits of joining. And although the number of benefits you offer may have some allure, the perceived meaningfulness of member benefits matters most. Most members would prefer two or three meaningful benefits rather than two dozen that have little or no value. Make time to evaluate your chamber's benefits periodically. Ask members and would-be members what matters most to them.

Promote Member Businesses With Website of the Month Feature

Visit the website for the South Wayne County Regional Chamber (Taylor, MI) and you'll notice a feature that highlights an individual member's website.

Chamber staff select one member's website to feature on the chamber homepage each month, says Sandy Mull, vice president. Doing so, she says, both encourages members to create a website that promotes their business and brings them more attention.

Chamber staffers rate member sites on appearance, user-friendliness and if a site entices a visitor to want to go beyond the homepage. Mull recommends having clear rules for the selection process so that members who are not selected do not feel slighted.

The chamber also allows members to nominate sites they feel are worthy of attention. Members can even nominate their own sites, but a member website can only be featured once every 12 months.

"We're always looking for services we can provide for our members," says Mull. "Website of the Month is just one more way to promote our member's businesses."

Source: Sandy Mull, Vice President, South Wayne County Regional Chamber, Taylor, MI. E-mail: Sandy@swcrc.com

Offer Members a Way to Recognize Key Staff

Allow your members a way to honor their staff by offering an award that lets them extol the virtues of their key employees or co-workers. This added-value benefit will strengthen your membership package.

The Northern Kentucky Chamber of Commerce (Fort Mitchell, KY) offers its 1,900 members a positive way to honor their key personnel. Through its Outstanding Administrative Professional of the Year Award, chamber members nominate administrative staff for recognition. All nominees are treated at the annual Administrative Professionals Breakfast held on Administrative Professionals Day.

The 2010 event, was the "fourth year giving out the award and the third year holding the event," says Tara Sorrell Proctor, coordinator of workforce, education and health care solutions at the chamber. "We typically receive 40 to 50 nominations each year. Members love nominating their administrative assistants, because it's a way of recognizing their hard work. The administrative professionals, even those who don't win the award, are honored just to be nominated."

The winner, honored at the annual breakfast event, receives a plaque and prizes valued at more than $200.

The chamber advertises the event on the home page of its website, at chamber meetings and events, through chamber-related e-mails and a contact list of administrative professionals the chamber has built over the last five years.

"Our judging process involves a panel of human resources professionals, as well as the previous year's Outstanding Administrative Professional of The Year winner," says Sorrell Proctor. "They are handed the essay portions of the nomination forms. We remove names and company affiliations, so that the process is as objective as possible.

To view the online nomination form for the administrative professional of the year award presented by the Northern Kentucky Chamber of Commerce (Fort Mitchell, KY), go to www.nkychamber.com and click on the link, Nominate Your Administrative Professional.

"It is still extremely difficult to choose a winner, as there are so many hard-working, dedicated and reliable administrative professionals in our community," she notes. "But in the end, the judges choose one person who has seemed to go above and beyond any reasonable expectations."

Source: Tara Sorrell Proctor, Coordinator, Workforce, Education & Health Care Solutions, Northern Kentucky Chamber of Commerce, Fort Mitchell, KY. E-mail: tsorrell@nkychamber.com

Membership Management Essentials for Chambers of Commerce

Use Member Numbers to Offer Group Benefits

At the Toledo Regional Chamber of Commerce (Toledo, OH), member benefits include health insurance, workers' compensation group pooling, office supply discounts and the opportunity to join its Member2Member (M2M) program, which allows the chamber's 2,773 members to offer one another business discounts.

Participating members can list discounts at the chamber website for an additional fee ($50 for text only, $75 for bold-type text and $100 for bold text plus logo).

Currently 25 members list discounts at the website, with all but three choosing the $100 logo listing option.

The program promotes members doing business with other members and adds value to the membership through the discounts, says Stacey Mallett, vice president of membership and marketing. "It also allows the chamber to address the requests we receive to provide a member benefit program without the additional stipulations we have for being considered a preferred provider, which include tracking and reporting, exclusivity in the market and revenue stream for the organization."

Mallett says one M2M member discount is promoted each week in the chamber's eInsider e-newsletter, which goes to 5,000 potential customers.

Source: Stacey Mallett, Vice President Membership and Marketing, Toledo Regional Chamber of Commerce, Toledo, OH. E-mail: Stacey.mallett@toledochamber.com

Sweeten the Pot With New Member Benefits

Freebies can be the shiny penny that turns people's heads toward your organization and entices them to want to learn more.

While advertisers have long known that people like to get more than they paid for, increasing numbers of member organizations are capitalizing on the universal desire by offering special benefits to first-time members.

"They are an enticement, but they also answer a question," says Kristin Gregory, executive director of the Carbondale (IL) Chamber of Commerce, of the complimentary benefits her organization has long provided to new members. "They are a tangible answer to the question of how the chamber serves its members in practical ways."

The chamber's benefits to new members (see box, below) provide something for everyone, but give particular attention to the needs of new or newly relocated business owners, says Gregory. Advertising services, free business consultations and discounted member services are consistently popular with new members, but chamber officials are always seeking new ideas from both current members and members of the chamber's board of directors.

Though membership incentives are directed primarily toward recruiting new members, current members benefit from these incentives, too. By donating benefits — most of the chamber's incentives are provided by current members — businesses raise awareness of their services and make positive connections with professionals who may become clients.

While few, if any, members join the chamber expressly to take advantage of first-time benefits, the incentives do help attract potential members and encourage them to sign on, says Gregory. "They are a bonus that adds value in members' minds, and for that we're glad to offer them. It's just another way to show that we're doing whatever we can for members."

Source: Kristin Gregory, Executive Director, Carbondale Chamber of Commerce, Carbondale, IL. E-mail: kristingregory@gmail.com

---

New Member Benefits Offered
By Carbondale (IL) Chamber of Commerce

- ❑ $100 free advertising in The Southern Illinoisan with purchase of $100
- ❑ Free commercial production with placement of advertising schedule on WPSD-TV
- ❑ 25 percent off purchase of advertising from one of the Wither's Radio stations
- ❑ Free business consultation with Feirich/Mager/Green/Ryan Law Firm
- ❑ 30 minutes free business counseling by Gilbert, Huffman, Prosser, Hewson & Barke
- ❑ Free mailbox for one year at Mail Boxes Etc.
- ❑ $0 down, $39.99 dues at Gold's Gym
- ❑ Buy 1 get 1 half price Annual Banquet tickets (Limit 1)
- ❑ 1 free insert in *"The Communicator"*
- ❑ 1 free Monthly Member Luncheon ticket
- ❑ 1 free member list or mailing labels

Buy Here Program Strengthens Membership

To achieve a successful membership base, it's important to support the success of each individual member. And if you can celebrate and boost your community while doing so, your efforts will have far-reaching impact.

The Iowa City Area Chamber of Commerce (Iowa City, IA) offers a Buy Here program that benefits both members and the Iowa City region.

Through the program, local business members are encouraged to shift 5 percent of their out-of-area spending to Iowa City area businesses.

Chamber officials report that this shift has created a stronger membership base while fostering a brotherhood among its 170 participating members and area business owners and strengthening the local economy.

In the first year after the implementation of the program, the Iowa City area gained back $1.1 million worth of business, chamber officials say. They anticipate the program will bring back a cumulative $95 million to the area over its duration.

"We live in a re-order world," says Rebecca Neades, vice president and director of public policy. "Sometimes there's a disconnect between a store manager and a purchasing manager."

To overcome this and relink local businesses, Neades works directly with area business owners to find local matches for business-to-business purchasing.

She notes that the program dispels the idea that local businesses cannot be competitive in bidding and pricing: "That's often a perception and not reality," she says.

Neades and her colleagues at the chamber offer the following suggestions to local business owners when aligning business purchases with the Buy Here program:

1. **Shift product purchases.** Convince members to shift purchases such as office supplies to a local vendor. Accounting for the lack of shipping costs, local vendors can be as competitive as discount suppliers.

2. **Shift service purchases.** Shift consumables such as banking, legal, accounting, 401K management, website development and hosting, public relations and more.

3. **Shift the obvious.** Consumables such as office cleaning supplies, printed materials and ad specialties are readily available locally and can be delivered without added shipping costs.

4. **Shift the subtle.** Shift your company credit card or gas card to a local bank or institution.

5. **Shift the unique.** Ask members what's unique in their business that could be purchased locally.

Neades says each participating member is asked to complete an online pledge form showing his/her support and participation in the program. This step ensures a sense of commitment to the program, she notes.

Chamber staff also heavily promote the program and include the pledge form with annual dues statements. For example, Neades says, the Buy Here program is not only addressed at each member visit, but is prominently featured at the chamber's website and in its advertising campaign.

Sources: Rebecca Neades, Vice President and Director of Public Policy; and Kelly McCann, Director of Communications, Iowa City Area Chamber of Commerce, Iowa City, IA. Phone (319) 337-9637. E-mail: rebecca@iowacityarea.com or kelly@iowacityarea.com

---

Member Talks Positively About Buy Here Program

What are members of the Iowa City Area Chamber of Commerce (Iowa City, IA) saying about its Buy Here program?

Monica Nadeau, general manager, Coral Ridge Mall (Coralville, IA) and a chamber member, has made a concerted effort to shift 5 percent of out-of-area purchases to the local region.

Doing so has been quite simple, Nadeau notes.

While she now is seeking a local vendor to supply new food trays, the first step in the mall's participation in the Buy Here program was to find a local supplier for parts and service of the mall's Zamboni machine used at its ice arena.

"We always assumed that because this is such a specialty item, we had to go through the Zamboni company," Nadeau says. "But we were able to find a local supplier for parts and service."

Nadeau has taken the effort a step further, successfully encouraging mall tenants — even those who are national retailers — to shift away from using contractors outside the region when opening a new store.

"I've been able to refer local contractors to these major retailers for bidding on construction jobs, and they've been chosen on numerous occasions because of their competitive pricing," Nadeau says, adding, "Local contractors don't have hotel stays, travel costs and other expenses that outside contractors have to build into their bid."

With the flooding in the area, Nadeau says the Buy Here program was more important than ever as it helped with matching local business owners and residents with local providers to assist them with emergency needs.

Monica Nadeau, General Manager, Coral Ridge Mall, Coralville, IA. E-mail: monica.nadeau@gpp.com

Area Maps Provide Varied Advertising Options

Give members the opportunity to advertise on widely used outreach materials.

Officials with the New Albany Chamber of Commerce (New Albany, OH) began producing area maps to include in their Welcome to New Albany packets in 2002. Printed versions, produced every three years, contain ads from member businesses. The online version, listed on the chamber's website, features hotlinks to member websites.

"The map project is a very important branding tool for the chamber," says Eileen Leuby, president. "It helps serve our mission, which is to promote our business community."

The project takes about 90 days, Leuby says. Hampton Publishing (www.hamptonpublish.com) handles the sale and placement of ads and printing.

"Our tasks are mailing the initial letters to members inviting them to advertise on the map, promoting the map project at our meetings/events, referring the inquiries to the sales rep, and allowing the sales rep to use our office to make calls and collect faxes during the project," she says.

Chamber staff proof the map design and create the map cover (shown at right).

In 2005, the chamber grossed $19,000 in sales from ad space on the maps, with 75 percent going to the publishing firm. For the 2008 version of the map, chamber officials anticipated costs would account for roughly 80 percent of map sales.

The 2005 map featured 25 display ads and 35 basic listing ads.

"Display ads are available on the back of the map," says Leuby. "Ads can be purchased in quarter panels, half panels and full panels. Members can also buy a simple basic listing ad which is in the directory on the back of the map. These basic listings are placed into categories, such as realtors, insurance, etc."

Plans were to print 25,000 of the 2008 version of the map. Advertising members receive free copies based on the amount of ad space they purchased. In addition, members who advertise on the map have the option of pre-ordering copies at a discounted price of $1 per map. After the maps are printed the cost is $2.95 each. The basic ads start at $79, with the addition of adding a hotlink to the member's website on the online version of the map costing another $25.

Content not available in this edition

"Members like the fact that there is a printed map and that they will be on the website with hotlink functions for website viewers to utilize," says Leuby. "Many people already have GPS systems in the car and/or use MapQuest to get map data. This extra feature of adding hotlinks makes the map participation more desirable."

Source: Eileen D. Leuby, President, New Albany Area Chamber of Commerce, New Albany, OH.

Kiosks Provide Unique Advertising Opportunity

Looking to provide your members with a far-reaching advertising tool? Consider offering kiosk advertising services.

Staff with the Tri-State Chamber of Commerce (Lakeville, CT) began working with Kiosk Advertising LLC a year ago to negotiate a special rate for chamber members — 10 percent off the $199 monthly fee.

Currently, about 10 chamber members run kiosk ads. The service is listed as a member benefit on the chamber website and in the membership newsletter.

In addition, "the chamber runs its own ad on the kiosks with our logo, byline and website address," says Sandy Gomez, secretary.

Twenty kiosk locations are available to members throughout the chamber's service area, including seven in member establishments. The flat LCD screens vary from 14 to 42 inches in size, depending on host location. Ads are eight to 10 seconds and run on an eight-minute loop.

Members can submit their artwork, photos and text to Kiosk Advertising to be used in the ads. Some ads are simply text accompanied by a logo, while others include photos and other graphics.

The kiosk ads grab attention, says Gomez, who adds: "A color visual is sometimes far better than a regular print ad or printed copy when promoting a service or event. It is also a great value."

Source: Sandy Gomez, Secretary, Tri-State Chamber of Commerce, Lakeville, CT. E-mail: info@tristatechamber.com

Create an Online Advertising Service

Offer members a high-tech perk: Advertising space on your website.

In 2008, staff with the Monroeville/Monroe County Chamber (Monroeville, AL) began offering members the option of purchasing advertising space through the chamber's website. Members can choose from seven advertising options, from a homepage banner ad ($500 annually) to a relocation page ad ($420 annually).

ECTown USA (Quincy, CA) designed the page on the chamber's website that showcases online advertising options, says Sandy Smith, chamber executive director. The website design company, Appleby Arts (Boulder City, NV) creates the member ads. Cost to create each ad is $30 without flash and $60 with flash.

The chamber's goal was to sell $3,000 in banner ads within the following year.

"The online advertising is a great opportunity for us to promote our local businesses, events and organizations, and everything is just a click away," says Smith.

Plans are to create a promotional campaign using radio, newspaper and online mediums to make all members aware of the new online advertising system, she says.

Smith emphasizes finding the right company to work with when designing an online advertising system for your members: "Find a company that is customer responsive and that specializes in your type of business. One reason we chose ECTown is that they do a lot of work with chambers. They wake up every day thinking of ways that chambers can assist their members and be a better front door to their communities."

Source: Sandy Smith, Executive Director, Monroeville/Monroe County Chamber, Monroeville, AL.

Key Chain Tag Serves as Convenient Benefit Reminder

Many organizations issue membership cards for members to use as identification. Why not issue cards for other purposes?

Since 1996, members of the Newport County Chamber of Commerce (Middletown, RI) have enjoyed a Member-2-Member discount program, taking advantage of available discounts at participating businesses by showing their chamber member key chain tags.

Content not available in this edition

"Once we started the discount program, we quickly realized that there was so much diversity in the types of discounts that we needed a physical thing to give members so that they would take advantage of them," says Jody J. Sullivan, deputy director.

Tags, given free to members, are created by a chamber member who runs a printing business. They are picked up at the chamber office or delivered by staff.

New members receive their discount tag in their welcome packets.

When the program began, members were invited to participate via letter, e-blast and phone calls. Today, new members are asked to participate when they join the chamber. Staff also advertise this program to members and the public as a major component of the chamber's "buy local" campaign.

Currently, 162 chamber members offer discounts to other members through the program.

Chamber staff order thousands of key chain tags annually In fall 2008, for instance, they ordered 10,000 tags at a cost of $2,119.

"Having the physical key tag on your key chain reminds you to use the discounts and keeps the chamber on your mind," says Sullivan. "It also shows the members giving the discount that we are driving business to them."

Versatile key chain tags can also be used in place of traditional membership cards or for benefits such as permanent parking passes for your lifetime members.

Source: Jody J. Sullivan, Deputy Director, Newport County Chamber of Commerce, Middletown, RI.
E-mail: jodyjude@newportchamber.com

Corporate Partnership Creates Member Toolkit Option

Partnering with major companies to offer workshops that provide meaningful, practical solutions to your members can assist them in building and thriving in business, adding value to memberships.

The Tucson Metropolitan Chamber of Commerce (Tucson, AZ) started offering members access to an online Small Medium Enterprise (SME) toolkit. Potential entrepreneurs and small business owners and managers who want to advance their operations participated in a free workshop introducing the toolkit.

This toolkit is a compendium of articles, software and business forms in a single, easy-to-use website that gives emerging and existing business owners a ready source for information to help steer their businesses.

A sample of the information the toolkit offers includes:

- Pragmatic advice, such as 10 things you can do to increase your cash flow, plus downloadable business forms, including sample business plans, time sheets, collection letters and materials on seeking financing.
- Reality-based information for potential business owners, such as Starting a Business Checklist, The Characteristics of a Successful Entrepreneur, specific points when buying a franchise and the realities of Web marketing.
- Specific tips for family-, minority- and women-owned businesses.

"We believe that the SME Toolkit gives business owners and managers the information they need to help their businesses thrive, not merely survive," says Jack Camper, chamber president. "We're pleased to partner with IBM in bringing this free and immediately useful tool to the entire Southern Arizona business community."

Learn more at: www.smetoolkit.com

Source: Jack Camper, Chamber President, Tucson Metropolitan Chamber of Commerce, Tucson, AZ.
E-mail: jcamper@tucsonchamber.org

Focus Efforts on Acquiring Added Benefits for Members

Partner with local businesses to add value and visibility to your membership.

Officials with the Knoxville Chamber of Commerce (Knoxville, TN) work to acquire business partnerships that will result in added benefits for its members.

In 2009, officials with the Knoxville Chamber of Commerce (Knoxville, TN) and Cellular Sales of Knoxville, Inc. (Knoxville, TN) announced a unique partnership that provides Chamber members with access to wireless technology and training. Together, the organizations work to grow regional businesses and ensure that the workforce is technologically advanced. In an unprecedented move, the chamber announced that Cellular Sales will be the Knoxville Chamber's "Official Wireless Sponsor."

"This opportunity to work with such a reputable member of our business community is a benefit to us and to our members," says Michelle Kiely, director of membership development at the chamber. "The chamber and its staff require reliable means of communication in and out of the office to maintain the highest level of customer support and service. This partnership affords the staff and chamber members the opportunity to learn more about how mobile connectivity can make us all more productive."

Kiely says working with the nation's largest Verizon wireless carrier that has the greatest market share in this region makes sense for the chamber, and that accessing business tools and services for its members is a priority among the chamber staff.

Source: Michelle Kiely, Chamber Director of Membership Development, Knoxville Chamber of Commerce, Knoxville, TN. E-mail: mkiely@knoxvillechamber.com

Business Partnership Tips

Michelle Kiely, director of membership development at the Knoxville Chamber of Commerce (Knoxville, TN), shares tips for collaborating with major retailers to score member discounts:

- ❑ Give careful consideration to the selection of sponsor prospects, making sure they would gain from the sponsorship and that the partnership aligns with your mission and goals.
- ❑ Do the research. Know as much about their business as you can — locations, target market and potential growth.
- ❑ Tailor the partnership presentation for a clear return on investment for both the sponsor and for your members; create a win-win relationship.

Membership Management Essentials for Chambers of Commerce

Offer Member Travel Tours

In October 2010, the Spearfish Area Chamber of Commerce (Spearfish, SD) offered its first overseas trip to China, with some 35 people from its membership and the community taking part.

Chamber officials are using lessons learned in that outing to enhance the next experience, a trip to the French Riviera this year, says Lisa Langer, executive director. Langer shares tips for planning a travel tour for members for the first time:

- Work with a reputable tour wholesaler. The chamber connected with travel wholesalers, Citslinc International (Monterey Park, CA) for the China excursion and Chamber Discoveries (Fresno, CA) for the French Riviera tour.
- Consider objections to buying local when planning an overseas trip. Chamber members instinctively have a buy local attitude, and a trip overseas could challenge this mentality.
- Take advantage of marketing efforts offered by the tour company, including brochures, flyers and ads.
- Consider having a pre-tour reception to discuss travel tips for the specific country or area you are visiting.

Source: Lisa Langer, Executive Director, Spearfish Area Chamber of Commerce & Visitor Center, Spearfish, SD.
E-mail: director@SpearfishChamber.org.

Members Speak Out Thanks to Membership Benefit

Add a special benefit to your membership package by offering a speakers bureau opportunity to members.

Adding a speakers bureau to your membership benefits not only offers members the opportunity to speak on their area of expertise, it also offers additional opportunities for member engagement and therefore promotes retention.

At the Colorado Women's Chamber of Commerce (CWCC) of Denver, CO, a speakers bureau was created to help members gain exposure. The speakers bureau is open to all chamber members who wish to be contacted for speaking engagements. The benefit has been a great way to help the members gain exposure and to help them succeed in their business ventures.

If you're considering a speakers bureau at your organization, follow these tips to get the initiative started off on the right foot:

- Add a Web page to your organization's website devoted to the speakers bureau where brief bios appear about participating speakers which outline their area of expertise and includes their contact information.
- Limit the scope of the bio of each speaker to about 250 words per person. The bios should be a snapshot of the speaker's experience and area of expertise, referred to as their "30-second commercial" at CWCC.
- Open participation in the speakers bureau to your members with the requirement that they consider opportunities to speak at organization events as a contribution to your mission.
- A speakers bureau is, of course, of benefit to members, but it can also be of value to the organization itself.

Source: Elizabeth Leake, Event and Project Manager, Colorado Women's Chamber of Commerce, Denver, CO. E-mail: eleake@cwcc.org

Meet Your Business Neighbor Events Facilitate Networking, Fun

At the New London Area Chamber of Commerce (New London, WI) networking opportunities are a key benefit for members who are aiming to promote their businesses. One opportunity the chamber offers is Meet Your Business Neighbor (MYBN), where members meet at local businesses for an evening of entertainment and mingling.

"What works best is when more than one member hosts an MYBN event," says Corinne Sommer, information specialist. "We encourage members to reach out to those members who have home-based businesses that don't necessarily have a storefront for exposure."

The chamber will soon be offering a Poker Run MYBN held at a variety of participating businesses where members have a chance to win prizes such as a plasma TV, gas grill package, wing party for 20 and a catered party for 20. This MYBN event will be a joint effort by six chamber members who are located in one geographic area.

Participants will visit each participating business for a stamp on their poker card. The event will end at one of the participating businesses where the poker hands will be dealt.

The best five poker hands will win the grand prizes, but there will be additional chances to win door prizes. A cookout and live music will round out the evening's festivities.

A variety of themes are offered at each monthly MYBN event. One of the most popular is the Music Trivia event held each January. Sommer explains the mechanics of this fresh and fun networking event:

- Chamber member businesses and organizations form teams of four or more to compete for a retro trophy.
- Teams hear a few minutes of a song and then have 30 seconds to name the song and artist before being given the next song.
- The team that answers the most songs and artists correctly wins the trophy and a year's worth of bragging rights.

The chamber's goal is to offer MYBN events monthly and involve approximately a fifth of the chamber's total membership.

Source: Corinne Sommer, Information Specialist, New London Area Chamber of Commerce, New London, WI.
E-mail: Corinne@newlondonwi.org

Membership Management Essentials for Chambers of Commerce

OFFER MANY AND VARIED NETWORKING OPPORTUNITIES

Those members who are more fully connected to and with other members generally find their association with a chamber to be more fulfilling. That's why it makes good sense to appeal to different groups by providing a variety of networking opportunities throughout the year: after hours, young professionals, meetings (both formal and informal), power meals, gender-specific events and more.

Customized Social Networking Platform Connects Members

Content not available in this edition

Move over Facebook, the Salem Area Chamber of Commerce (Salem, OR) has Face2Face — a social network geared to the chamber's membership. Seven hundred and seventy of the chamber's 1,210 members currently utilize Face2Face to promote their events and businesses and to offer any business-related updates. Face2Face works similarly to Facebook: Members have their own profiles, can send status updates and share news.

Using the Ning Platform (www.ning.com), Kyle Sexton, director of business development, developed a customized platform that allows members to post updates within its own Salem Chamber network and more.

One component of the Face2Face network is Newshare, where members can post status updates related to their businesses. The Salem Chamber blog had previously served a similar function, but the Newshare terminology increased its use by 400 percent, said Sexton. While many members did not see the purpose in blogging, they could easily understand the term newshare,"which promoted use of this aspect of Face2Face.

Although the information available at Face2Face is public, only members can post to the site, making the offering exclusive, and therefore, a valuable benefit offered by the chamber.

Eventshare is another facet of the Face2Face network where members can post their events on a community calendar making the search capability convenient for anyone searching for events in the Salem area.

Each component of Face2Face — including Eventshare and Newshare — are integrated with other social platforms such as Twitter and Facebook. Therefore, all posts entered at Face2Face are automatically uploaded to Twitter and the chamber's Facebook page within 30 minutes. Additionally, Face2Face posts are also automatically sent to the Salem Chamber's website, which increases the search engine optimization of member businesses and posts.

The chamber offers one-on-one training, videos posted at the chamber's site and small group trainings throughout the year for $29 per person. The training and tutorials serve to aid members in learning about the new technology and how it will benefit their business.

To offer Face2Face to your members, you would need to access a platform like Ning (which costs approximately $200 per year) and build a customized platform. Working with a knowledgeable programmer to customize your platform can cost about $1,500.

View the Salem Area Chamber of Commerce's Face2Face network at http://face2face.salemchamber.org/.

Source: Kyle Sexton, Director of Business Development, Salem Area Chamber of Commerce, Salem, OR. E-mail: kyle@salemchamber.org

Making a Social Network Work

Are you interested in a social networking function for your members? Kyle Sexton, director of business development for Salem Area Chamber of Commerce ,shares the following tips when offering a social network for members:

- Make it clear to members why the social network exists and what the purpose of the service is. Post a user code of ethics and a list of good posting practices so the rules are clear.
- Find members with expertise to share and who understand the technology. Seek out members who truly understand the use and functionality of a social network and solicit their help in training others.
- Have serious consequences for abusers. If the rules of Face2Face are broken — such as using the service for spamming purposes — a user is barred from ever using the service again.

Membership Management Essentials for Chambers of Commerce

Take Steps to Maximize Member Receptions

In the past, staff with the Ann Arbor Area Chamber of Commerce (Ann Arbor, MI) typically hosted four member receptions each year. Because of the popularity of the gatherings, they doubled that number to eight this year.

With a membership of 1,350, the chamber attracts 125 to 150 members who gather for a night of socializing and networking at each reception, says Cheryl O'Brien, membership director. She offers tips for creating successful member receptions:

- **Limit the number of receptions so they don't become old hat.** Offering receptions too frequently can water down the effect of the event.

- **Advertise the event.** This chamber lists the event at the website's home page and event calendar, which receives 25,000 hits each month, and in a bi-weekly e-newsletter that goes to a list of 8,000. The chamber reaches an additional 10,000 people (both members and non-members) through a partnership with the Ann Arbor Business Review, a weekly business publication that includes a special chamber section called the B2B in the first publication of each month.

- **Do away with the old meet-and-greet tricks and allow your members a night of freedom to mingle.** O'Brien suggests saving the structured networking ideas for other member meetings. Have staffers and ambassadors watch for attendees standing alone to engage them in conversation and make them feel welcome.

- **Tour the reception site in advance.** O'Brien goes on-site to ensure the venue offers ample space, good flow for mingling and ample parking. The site host must also have been a chamber member in good standing for at least one year.

- **Meet at unusual locations.** This chamber has sponsored receptions at a performance theater, martini bar and exercise facility. The reception at the exercise facility included a game of basketball while a reception at Comcast included tours of the facility. O'Brien recommends making the night as memorable as possible.

- **Offer a hook.** Whether it's food from the best caterer in town or gift bags given to the first 100 guests, tangible rewards draw a crowd. O'Brien recalls one event hosted by a member spa where guests had personalized colognes mixed for them. The cost for prizes can be offset by obtaining a reception sponsor. This chamber asks a sponsor to donate $1,000 to the event. In turn, the sponsor receives recognition in the chamber's marketing of the event.

- **Make it a members-only event.** Non-members who see the advertised receptions frequently contact O'Brien about the events. After a conversation about membership, O'Brien easily gains a new member.

Source: Cheryl O'Brien, Membership Director, Ann Arbor Chamber of Commerce, Ann Arbor, MI. E-mail: Cheryl@annarborchamber.org

Combine a Meal With Programming, Networking

Serving seven small communities and 70 miles of interstate in Eastern Colorado, staff at the I-70 Corridor Chamber of Commerce (Bennett, CO) work hard to provide members with both professional development and networking opportunities.

One way they do so is through Lunch and Learn meetings that address local issues and general business needs, says Lois Buckman, secretary of the chamber's board of directors.

The monthly meetings draw 25 to 30 participants, about 20 percent of overall membership. Just as important, Buckman says, they consistently attract nonmembers who often end up joining the chamber.

Members and nonmembers alike can purchase lunch for $10, but the meetings themselves are free and open to the public. Past speakers have included both academics and local business authorities.

Recent presentation topics included the dos and don'ts of e-mail communication, logo and branding pointers, budget issues facing local school systems, and the impact of a new recreation center on area business.

But programming isn't everything. "Attendance also depends on what you're serving," Buckman says with a laugh. "It's not what you probably want to spend your time thinking about, but honestly, it does make a difference, so you might as well make sure it's something appealing."

Source: Lois Buckman, Secretary of the Board of Directors, I-70 Corridor Chamber of Commerce, Bennett, CO. E-mail: Admin@i70ccoc.com

Unique Touches Jazz Up After-hours Events

After-hours events are a staple of many member organizations. Creating events that are stimulating and unique helps increase attendance and create a more memorable experience for members.

Ashleigh Bates, operations manager, Carmel Chamber (Carmel, IN), shares some of the creative ways chamber staff add pizzazz to their after-hours events:

✓ **Raffle off gift certificates relevant to the host.** When an event is hosted at a restaurant, for example, the chamber will purchase a gift certificate from the restaurant and raffle it off at the event.

✓ **Be more creative about event locations.** Last winter the chamber staff held an event at a new spa. "People were curious about the renovations that had gone on there, so we had a great turnout," she says.

✓ **Have more interactive events.** Several of the chamber's businesses are located in a large outdoor mall. For one after-hours event, they offered a walkthrough where members could visit more than 15 businesses in two hours. Each participating business had food, drinks or giveaways.

✓ **Have members partner with each other for events.** Bates says they have members who want to host an event but who aren't used to working with food and refreshments, or who may want to partner with another member to present it. In these cases, they match them with a member caterer willing to provide the food and drink, if they provide the location. Both members share the recognition for the event.

✓ **Make events annual.** Every November, a local florist hosts an after-hours event, decorating the store differently than the year before, which has members looking forward to what they will do next. The florist partners with a member jeweler at the same shopping center, and members mingle between the two locations all night.

Source: Ashleigh Bates, Operations Manager, Carmel Chamber, Carmel, IN. E-mail: ab@carmelchamber.com

Five-minute Networking Maximizes Membership

Ever tried speed dating? The concept is simple, fast and fun: Men and women meet to mix and mingle, individuals of one gender stay seated at a table-for-two while members of the other gender move from table to table every five minutes.

The result? Everyone makes lots of contacts and each person can determine whether to take a relationship further at a later time.

Following that concept to introduce members with one another for business networking purposes rather than romance, staff with Greater Louisville Inc.-The Metro Chamber of Commerce (Louisville, KY) offer the Five-Minute Networking Program to assist 2,700 members in maximizing and growing their business network.

The chamber promotes five-minute networking events as an innovative, effective way for members to network in a fast-paced, professional relationship-building experience.

At the event, members sit in two rows, one group on side A of a table, another on side B. Every five minutes, the group rotates so each person is across from a new face.

With 60 to 80 members at each networking event, members are guaranteed to meet at least 10 business contacts at each event. The chamber offers sessions in the morning, evening and after business hours in order to reach the most interested members.

"The way this works is that it makes you get right to the point and talk about your business," says Jennifer Ball, director of creative services at the chamber.

Specialized software by 5MinuteNetworking Software (www.5minutenetworking.com) allows the chamber to match members with others in industries that would complement their business and that will assist in marketing their business needs.

"Those attending the sessions not only meet many business connections, but they also make many referrals for other members," says Ball.

Consider offering five-minute networking events that enable members to connect within your organization. Follow these tips for making your networking event a success:

❑ Educate your members and offer them tips to maximize their experience.

❑ Encourage members to avoid attending each and every networking event. With a constant influx of new and potential members, members will gain more by attending every other session to gain exposure to more new members at one time.

❑ Partner with other membership organizations within your community — such as young professional networks or women's business groups — to strengthen the networking possibilities.

Source: Jennifer Ball, Director of Creative Services, Greater Louisville Inc.-The Metro Chamber of Commerce, Louisville, KY. E-mail: JBall@greaterlouisville.com

Attract New Audiences With Off-hours Networking

Consider offering member meetings and other events at different times to draw new and diverse sets of attendees.

The Faribault Area Chamber of Commerce & Tourism (Faribault, MN) not only features Business After Hours meetings for evening networking opportunities, it offers early morning meetings as well. With a solid membership of 475 active members, chamber officials say they find offering Business Before Hours membership meetings at 7:30 a.m. weekdays to be as well-attended as those offered after regular business hours.

By offering meetings at nonstandard times, more members can be reached, says Kymn Anderson, president of the chamber. "Our members see the value in attending, learning more about the host business and sharing information with all who attend," she explains. "We also change the topic now and then, to allow businesses to give a testimonial or ask for a referral. The host also makes an effort to invite their neighbors, colleagues and vendors to benefit from the event."

Anderson offers tips for attracting strong attendance at early morning networking meetings:

1. **Continue consistent standards.** Chamber staff bring to these early morning meetings the same tools they find effective at after-hours meetings. According to Anderson, the opportunity for self-promotion has been the best attraction for Business Before Hours. By offering a networking portion of the meeting where attendees can make announcements, members experience the early-bird-gets-the-worm theory. Anderson says these early morning announcements facilitate leads and referrals between members that reinforce the importance of supporting local businesses.

2. **Create a relaxed early morning atmosphere.** Make things easy on members by scheduling morning meetings on a consistent day and time. Keep standards of dress informal and casual to make everyone feel comfortable, especially any newcomers who might be attending. Have greeters assigned to guarantee everyone is included and is introduced. This expedites the morning meeting and helps get everyone off to work on time.

Source: Kymn Anderson, President, Faribault Area Chamber of Commerce & Tourism, Faribault, MN. E-mail: kymn@faribaultmn.org.

Let Members Rub Elbows With Elected Officials

At the Greater Indianapolis Chamber of Commerce (Indianapolis, IN), networking has reached an entirely new level. The Chamber's HobNob event allows members to rub elbows with elected officials.

HobNob connects members with political candidates in election years and elected officials in nonelection years. Held in the fall, the chamber promotes this event as the premiere political event in Central Indiana, opening the political season and offering a casual social atmosphere.

HobNob gathers candidates for the upcoming election year in a public, non-partisan, environment and provides both chamber and community members the opportunity to interact one-on-one with candidates, says Cara Klaer, communications specialist.

"Attendees engage in important discussion with elected officials, business leaders and community members," says Klaer. "The goal is to educate the public to make an informed decision on Election Day, and ultimately influence change in the community."

"We are told members like the fact that HobNob gathers politicians, their strategists and the people who cover them all in one place," says Klaer.

Try these tips for hosting a meaningful HobNob event for your members:

- Ask city council members and the mayor to join the event. This year's HobNob will feature candidates for the city-county council and mayor.

- Prepare a substantive question and answer period for the audience to interact with candidates in a significant way. Local Indiana political candidates participate in a question and answer session at HobNob, focused on key issues like economic growth, transportation, fiscal policy and education. In years past, HobNob proved to be a flashpoint for candidates for Marion County prosecutor and provided an early glimpse of Mayor Greg Ballard, who went on to stage one of the biggest election upsets in Indiana political history, says Klaer.

- Have political candidates wear nametags that clearly identify them and what post they are vying for or hold. This ensures that there are no embarrassing mistakes in identity when an attendee is approaching a political candidate.

Source: Cara Klaer, Communications Specialist, and Donna M. Marino, Senior Vice President of Sales and Marketing, Greater Indianapolis Chamber of Commerce, Indianapolis, IN. E-mail: DMarino@indylink.com

Membership Management Essentials for Chambers of Commerce

Host Successful Member Breakfast Meetings

Consistently bringing together your members can nurture the bonds they have with one another and with your cause.

Staff with the Hartford Area Chamber of Commerce (Hartford, WI), in conjunction with two other chambers in Washington County, coordinate a monthly breakfast meeting for members to network and share ideas. The event is dubbed the Washington County Interactive Networking (WIN) Member Breakfast Meeting. Event costs are covered by fees to attend — $10 for members and $20 for nonmembers.

Kim Infalt, executive director, answers a few questions about the breakfast meeting:

Why are breakfast meetings like this so important?

"These meetings go a step beyond After Hours gatherings most chambers host. We hold the meetings from 7:30 to 9 a.m., and it's here where members network and discuss issues relevant to their businesses and still have time to put in a full day at work."

How many members attend and how do you get the word out about this event?

"We average 40 to 55 members at each breakfast. We start getting the word out early in the month about the upcoming breakfast and particularly speak to new members about the event, encouraging them to participate. It's also posted in our newsletter."

What unique things do you do during the breakfast meetings?

"Each member is encouraged to give a 30-second commercial about their business ... to start the networking process. We typically have a guest speaker as well, usually a member who speaks on a relevant business topic. ... Members share success stories and 'most outrageous business requests.' Whether they're looking for an employee, office equipment or have a technical question, they can express that here."

What keeps the members coming to these events?

"Members see the importance of networking and building strong business relationships. We also select a new venue each month that can hold at least 50 people. The event is always held at a chamber member's restaurant or other business location. When not held at a restaurant, the event is catered by a chamber member and held at another member's location such as the bank or golf course."

What do members say about this monthly event?

"Because we partner this meeting with two other area chambers within our county, the members get to meet many new people they wouldn't ordinarily meet. This offers them a broader networking scope, which they like, and it helps their businesses grow. Our goal is to keep business local and within the county."

Source: Kim Infalt, Executive Director, Hartford Area Chamber of Commerce, Hartford, WI. E-mail: kim@hartfordchamber.org

Invite Celebrities to Speak at Your Member Breakfasts

If you have staff or members connected to the rich and famous, look for ways those relationships can benefit your cause.

Staff with the Middlesex County Chamber of Commerce (Middletown, CT) capitalize on connections their members and their chamber president — who played with the American Football League's New York Titans in the 1960s — have with well-known individuals in national political and athletic sectors.

Larry McHugh, president and former Titan, says monthly chamber breakfasts feature celebrity speakers who can talk on issues relevant to the county and connect with local business leaders.

Past speakers include National Basketball Association players Ray Allen and Kevin Ollie; University of Connecticut Men's Basketball Coach Jim Calhoun; Major League Baseball's Jeff Bagwell; actor/writer/producer Joe Pantoliano; President Bill Clinton; Rev. Jesse Jackson and U.S. Sen. Christopher Dodd.

McHugh says because the monthly breakfasts usually draw a crowd of 500-plus, they host the events at a hotel with a meeting room capable of holding up to 1,000 people. Cost, including breakfast, is $18 for chamber members and $28 for nonmembers.

"Not only does our member breakfast provide our members with the opportunity to hear a well-known speaker," says McHugh, "it also provides them a great networking opportunity because of the large crowd the breakfast draws."

They promote the member breakfasts through a monthly mailer, promotional flyers sent to the membership and through all media outlets.

Source: Larry McHugh, President, Middlesex County Chamber of Commerce, Middletown, CT. E-mail: lmchugh@middlesexchamber.com

Make Celebrity Connections

Larry McHugh, president, Middlesex Chamber of Commerce (Middletown, CT), shares strategies to connect with celebrities for your next member event:

- **Rely on your background.** McHugh stays in touch with colleagues from high school, college and his career as a professional football player.

- **Use affiliations with other associations** (professional, hobbies, etc.) to network and form personal relationships with prospective speakers.

- **Ask members.** You never know what connections they may have that could lead to a great guest.

- **Make yourself available** at other events that feature celebrity speakers, introducing yourself and asking if they would speak at your event.

Golf Provides Format for Networking, Sponsorships

Hosting a golf outing provides a chance to get members together in a nontraditional way, outside of restaurants and meeting rooms.

Staff with the Winona Area Chamber of Commerce (Winona, MN) hosted its 9th Annual Golf Outing this past summer, says Shannon Schell, membership services coordinator.

The popular event, Schell says, "is a wonderful opportunity to entertain business associates and to make new business connections." Members are invited to bring a client to the outing, which helps builds relationships, as well.

"It's a fun day," Schell says. "We have a lot of prizes and giveaways at almost every hole."

Chamber staff invite members to purchase a sponsorship for $80 at the golf outing. "Sponsors get their company's name on a sign at a hole, and we also thank them in our newsletter," Schell says. "It's a good way for a smaller business to get their name out there."

Each January, a four-person committee starts seeking donations and sponsorships for the June event. A list of potential and regular contributors is compiled, and they are then contacted by telephone, says Schell, who notes: "It goes smoothly, because many of the sponsors plan to contribute each year."

Approximately 130 people attend the golf outing each summer. It's a four-person team event, so teams of members may sign up together. Members also may be placed with a team, which is another good opportunity to network.

The event is a successful fundraiser, says Schell, noting that proceeds support the chamber's general budget fund.

Registration fee is $80 per person, which includes 18 holes of golf, cart rental, dinner and prizes. Dinner only is offered for non-golfers at $20 per person, which is another way to attract more people to the event.

Source: Shannon Schell, Membership Services Coordinator, Winona Area Chamber of Commerce, Winona, MN.
E-mail: slschell@winonachamber.com

Look for Ways to Engage Members, Despite Weather

If you live in an area where winter is already tightening its icy grip, give your members something to look forward to that embraces and celebrates the weather.

Whether it's an outdoor softball tournament, a group hike in a local nature area or an organization-sponsored outing to an area sledding and ski spot, offer fun opportunities to members and potential members. Carry the fun back indoors with a reception featuring hot chocolate, cappuccino and fresh cookies as a chance to mix and mingle as participants warm up following the outdoor adventure.

You can even put a wintry spin on your organization's annual golf tournament by hosting a midwinter golf outing. This is what the Harrison Chamber of Commerce (Harrison, MI) has done for the past 20 years.

"The idea for the Frostbite Open was developed when a group of local golfers wanted something fun to do during the winter months," says Deb Gadberry, chamber president. "That idea has evolved into five, nine-hole courses set up on frozen Budd Lake."

The event is a two-person scramble where each golfer is assigned a tennis ball, a course and a hole. Gadberry says each golfer can use only three clubs (no woods) and must move around the course until all nine holes are played.

The event also features turkey bowling, a men's and women's longest drive competition and a closest-to-the-pin challenge.

The February 2008 event, saw 245 people participate to help the chamber raise funds for the Fourth of July fireworks show. Through registration fees ($15 per person), T-shirt sales, flag sponsors and 50/50 raffles, the event brought in around $2,700.

Source: Deb Gadberry, President, Harrison Chamber of Commerce, Harrison, MI.
E-mail: glamorize@yahoo.com

Tips for a Successful Winter Golf Event

The Harrison Chamber of Commerce (Harrison, MI), features a popular winter golf tournament for members, the Frostbite Open. Here, Deb Gadberry, president, offers advice for member-based organizations looking to organize such an event:

- Designate a chairperson who is responsible for overseeing the entire event.

- Have at least 25 volunteers to assist the chairperson with various duties behind the scenes as well as the day of the event.

- Locate an area large enough to accommodate five nine-hole golf courses.

- If your event is going to be held on a lake, apply for a permit with your local city or county government to hold the event on ice.

- Have a good idea of how many golfers will attend prior to the day of the event.

- Design and order T-shirts for the participants.

- Create a master registration sheet, assigning all golfers to their respective courses/holes.

Chamber Gears Quarterly Events to Female Members

The Lakeville Area Chamber of Commerce (Lakeville, MN) hosts quarterly Women of the Lakeville Chamber Luncheons that regularly draw 60 to 90 attendees, says Linda Rynda, director of member services.

Rynda shares ways they keep this ongoing event fresh:

❏ **Rotate event formats.** Events rotate between three formats:

   ✓ **Progressive dinner event:** Temporary walls divide three areas of the room. The first section features appetizers and seating for attendees to sit and network. The next section features the main course, and members sit with different members. In the third section, attendees enjoy dessert as they sit with yet another group of chamber members.

   ✓ **Demonstration event:** Members participate in a cooking demonstration or similar hands-on learning event.

   ✓ **Guest speakers:** Twice a year, quarterly meetings involve presentations by special guest speakers or a panel of speakers. Topics, chosen with the audience in mind, may include issues such as financial awareness or management.

❏ **Spotlight sponsor specialties.** Ask members to sponsor each women-centric event by offering a special touch. For example, at one women's luncheon, a florist member gave each attendee a rose.

❏ **Avoid alienating male members.** Although the quarterly luncheon is geared to women, they welcome any male members interested in attending. Some Lakeville Chamber male members attend the women's quarterly luncheon to network, partly because their businesses cater to women.

❏ **Add an element of surprise.** Try event themes that are new and unusual for your members and be sure to include a fresh twist to icebreakers.

Source: Linda Rynda, Director of Member Services, Lakeville Area Chamber of Commerce and Convention & Visitors Bureau, Lakeville, MN.
E-mail: LindaR@lakevillechamber.org

Icebreakers Keep Members Mixing

Linda Rynda, director of member services, Lakeville Area Chamber of Commerce (Lakeville, MN), shares ways they encourage members to mingle at quarterly Women of the Lakeville Chamber Luncheons:

• Have members pass business cards and introduce themselves to others at their table within three minutes. Then, have members answer two prepared questions at the table, one related to personal sharing such as, "What was your favorite vacation?" and the other related to business such as, "What was your most successful marketing technique?"

• Play alphabet bingo. Distribute cards with nine blocks that contain letters. Ask members to mingle, marking off the first letter of other persons' last names on their card. Offer small prizes to those who can fill their card within a set time.

• Assign seats or pull names from a hat to randomly select who will sit by whom, encouraging mixing and networking.

Membership Management Essentials for Chambers of Commerce.
Edited by Scott C. Stevenson.
© 2012 Stevenson, Inc. Published 2012 by Stevenson, Inc.

Membership Management Essentials for Chambers of Commerce

MEMBER RECRUITMENT STRATEGIES

What are you doing to recruit members each year? Do you make a point to thoroughly evaluate your recruitment strageies? Are you continuing to test new recruitment strategies? Review these 11 different recruitment approaches used by chambers of varying sizes and locations throughout the nation.

Invite Members to Bring a Guest to Events

In the spring, staff with the Kansas City Kansas Area Chamber of Commerce (Kansas City, KS) asked their members to invite five or more potential members as their guests to two events during the chamber's membership drive.

Staff asked members to provide names and contact information of their guests in advance of each event. Any member who brought five or more guests total to the two events was entered into a drawing for a free advertising insert in the chamber newsletter as well as a quarter-page biography.

Janet Reed, director of sales, says the effort brought 25 new leads and resulted in 10 to 12 new members.

Members learned of the opportunity through announcements at events and in the chamber newsletter. Reed says the idea was developed out of a need to find a quick, inexpensive and fun way to obtain member referrals.

Source: Janet R. Reed, Director of Sales, Kansas City Kansas Area Chamber of Commerce, Kansas City, KS.

Member Campaign Includes Phonathon, Incentives

A recently launched marketing campaign by the Largo/Mid-Pinellas Chamber of Commerce (Largo, FL) is doing double duty as its membership campaign as well.

Your Region! Our Chamber! serves a dual purpose as the chamber's newly unveiled marketing initiative. In addition to being used in a direct mail and print advertising blitz for the next year, chamber staff developed four postcards (two are shown at right), each with a different member testimonial gathered for the marketing campaign.

"We identified around 300 target businesses in our service area and sent them a different card every three days over the course of two weeks," says Tom Morrissette, president.

The month-long membership campaign, A Treasure of Benefits, kicked off with a two-day phonathon where member volunteers contacted those target businesses. Teams of volunteers competed for prizes and recognition. Each time they brought in new members, they would draw from a treasure chest filled with prizes, from spa treatments to restaurant gift certificates. Top individual new member recruiter (in dollars) received a cruise; top individual new member recruiter (in numbers), a trip to an Orlando resort and tickets to SeaWorld; and top team new member recruiters (in dollars), a private suite stocked with food and drink to entertain 30 guests at a minor-league baseball game.

With a week left in the campaign, the chamber was nearing its goal of $20,000 in new membership revenue, with $18,000 already earned largely from the phonathon, says Morrissette, noting the marketing initiative is an important element to its success.

"While increasing the number of member associates and dollars to the organization is important, the ultimate goal from this campaign is for the chamber to have greater visibility in our service region, specifically in regards to the

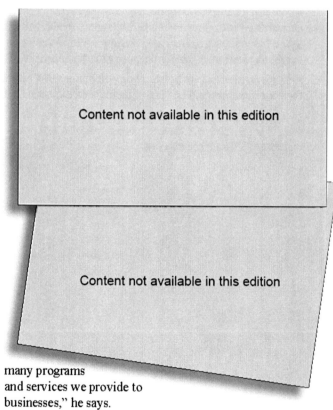

Content not available in this edition

Content not available in this edition

many programs and services we provide to businesses," he says.

In addition to the postcards, the new slogan will be used on membership applications, the chamber's newly launched website, in e-mails and on chamber billboards. Sponsors covered costs of the marketing and membership campaigns, including prizes.

Source: Tom Morrissette, President, Largo/Mid-Pinellas Chamber of Commerce, Largo, FL. E-mail: tom@largochamber.org

Membership Management Essentials for Chambers of Commerce

Business Card Exchange Strengthens Membership

A popular business card exchange has helped staff with the Eastern Montgomery County Chamber of Commerce (Jenkintown, PA) grow membership to 700.

Through the business card exchange events, staff encourage member interaction and build the database of potential members with information gleaned from the business cards. Members attend events for free and a group of prospective members is invited as well, both groups enticed by the prospect of winning prizes and enjoying great food.

Upon entering the event, attendees simply drop their business cards in a basket or bowl. Chamber staff use these cards for prize drawings and to garner contact information to promote membership to prospective members.

"We ask that our host partner with another member who is a caterer or restaurant to provide light refreshments for the attendees," says Nancy Ischinger, member services director. "The host also has an opportunity during the event to speak about their place of business and the services they offer."

Here are points to consider in creating your own business card exchange event:

- Boost attendance by making the event free for both current and prospective members.
- Host the event at a member's venue at no charge to the organization.
- Promote event heavily in area media, through e-mails and social networking sites.
- Make the event brief and offer light refreshments.
- Use business card information to build your database for prospective member contacts. Contact attendees immediately after the event to thank them and invite them to your next event.

Source: Nancy Ischinger, Member Services Director, Eastern Montgomery County Chamber of Commerce, Jenkintown, PA. E-mail: Nancy@emccc.org

Drive Yields $110,000, Draws 281 New Members

Three days, almost 300 volunteers, 281 new members and $110,000 in dues equal one successful membership drive, but you might not guess the most important ingredient of all: rock and roll.

"The Rock the Chamber theme created immense buzz in the business community," says Gayle Anderson, president and CEO of the Greater Winston-Salem Chamber of Commerce (Winston-Salem, NC). "I can't tell you how many people said to me, 'I've got to do this just to see what the heck is going on.'"

The interest generated around the peer-to-peer calling campaign was no accident. Chamber officials created a fictitious rock band and worked hard to promote it, with Anderson dressing in leather, carrying a guitar, and giving interviews as her rock superstar alter ego, Hurricane Anderson.

The theme was part of an overall strategy created in consultation with Your Chamber Connection, a Fort Worth, TX-based consultancy emphasizing fast-paced, high-energy events.

But while the drive was lighthearted fun for volunteers, it was careful planning and logistics for organizers. Twelve campaign captains were recruited from chamber members and commissioned to recruit five separate teams of volunteers. Each of the captains' teams was then assigned responsibility for one of the drive's five calling sessions.

In each two-and-a-half-hour session, volunteers were given a thorough orientation on how a chamber benefits businesses and how it can be sold to prospective members. The actual calling was done in a festive atmosphere of energizing music and cheering at each new membership.

"The Rock the Chamber theme created immense buzz in the business community."

Since the completion of the campaign, officials at many chambers of commerce have contacted Anderson. Her advice is always the same: Be willing to go all in or don't do it at all. She explains that the success of Rock the Chamber required her entire staff of 18 for a full week, with many additional hours beyond that.

She also advises trusting consultants. "If you are going to hire them in the first place, do exactly what they say," she says. "They have done this many times and know how to make it work, so just trust the advice they give you."

Source: Gayle Anderson, President and CEO, Greater Winston-Salem Chamber of Commerce, Winston-Salem, NC. E-mail: anderson@winstonsalem.com

Membership Management Essentials for Chambers of Commerce

New Member Program Offers Financial Reward

At the TwinWest Chamber of Commerce (Plymouth, MN), existing members are encouraged to recruit new members. Chamber officials say the new member referral program is directly responsible for bringing in as many as 30 percent of the chamber's 1,000 members.

The program is simple: A current member refers a business, which in turn, makes a decision to join. The current member then receives a $35 credit to use toward the cost of a chamber program or event.

"This is a powerful and useful tool that benefits the chamber and, in turn, helps the local economy grow stronger by encouraging businesses to join the chamber," says Jacqui Sauter, regional sales director. "In this economic downturn, offering reimbursement for referrals allows the chamber to grow, and the reward is a nice benefit for members, too."

Consider these important points when introducing reimbursement for member referrals:

- Send a personal thank-you letter along with the monetary coupon to the referring member once the referred member officially joins.

- Allow the referring member to use the coupon within one year of receipt toward events or programs within your chamber.

- Acknowledge referrals in member communications. At the chamber, referring members are honored as TwinWest Champions on the membership page of its monthly magazine. This acknowledgement encourages others to participate in the program.

Source: Jacqui Sauter, Regional Sales Director, TwinWest Chamber of Commerce, Plymouth, MN. E-mail: jacqui@twinwest.com

Uncampaign Fills the Pipeline for Chamber Membership

It might sound counterproductive to call an annual membership growth campaign an UnCampaign, but it hasn't hindered the Jacksonville Regional Chamber of Commerce (Jacksonville, FL) in any way says Senior Manager, Member Relations Jennifer Strickland.

"The UnCampaign allows us to keep a consistently full pipeline of prospects while also creating an extension of our sales force. Many times, a volunteer has done such a good job explaining the benefits of membership to a lead that our account managers have to spend little or no time selling the membership."

Current members volunteer to help find new members for the chamber. Volunteers receive one point for each dollar in new revenue they refer to the chamber, through leads they submit to a dedicated e-mail address.

Staff nominate team captains and the current campaign chair based on past performance and enthusiasm for the initiative. They are responsible for training and motivating their chosen team (see side story), as well as hosting at least two outside meetings or functions with their teams to review best practices and offer support. Captains are rewarded with extensive visibility for themselves and their businesses throughout the campaign.

All leads closed in a calendar year are given credit, though the UnCampaign itself runs just 16 weeks, from March to the end of June. During that time the chamber hosts a kick-off event, several reward sessions and a victory party to drive momentum.

Strickland says the campaign has done great things for their membership numbers. "Before the recent economic downturn, we were able to increase new membership revenue generated by volunteers by 74 percent. Even as the economy struggled, we were only 4 percent under our production through volunteers."

Source: Jennifer Strickland, Senior Manager, Member Relations, Jacksonville Regional Chamber of Commerce, Jacksonville, FL. E-mail: Jennifer.strickland@myjaxchamber.com

Ensure Fairness in Recruitment Competition By Enlisting a Draft

Senior Manager, Member Relations, Jennifer Strickland, Jacksonville Regional Chamber of Commerce (Jacksonville, FL) says their annual membership growth campaign, or UnCampaign as they call it, is nothing if not fair — partly because of a kick-off that includes an NFL-style draft, where team captains choose volunteers to help them reach their goals.

"Each captain has an equal opportunity to build a competitive team. Team captains draw from a hat to determine selection order and then proceed, in turn, to draft volunteers to their team. We use a 1-10-1 format for fairness; the volunteer who drew number ten goes first in the second round of the draft, giving them picks 10 and 11, and the first volunteer picks 1 and 20. We reverse order as such after each round. Volunteers are chosen based on past production or potential. Each team is challenged to produce an equal portion of the overall campaign goal."

Strickland says the draft provides captains with other benefits as well. "It allows them to become familiar with all of the volunteers in the program as they review the lists and make selections. This gives a better sense of community from the leadership throughout the campaign events. It also promotes a wider range of business connections."

Just because it's fair doesn't mean that everyone ends up happy though. "Not everyone ends up with their friends," says Strickland. "Though we never segregate teams at functions, some people would still prefer to be on the team of their favorite captain." In the end, however, many of them appreciate the new relationships they formed by stepping outside of their usual circles.

To help alleviate issues, Strickland says it's necessary to have as many rules as you can think of before beginning. "Having volunteers understand the parameters on the front end alleviates confusion when the money starts coming in."

Membership Management Essentials for Chambers of Commerce

Chamber Grows by 87 Members in One Week

The Mount Vernon-Lee Chamber of Commerce (Alexandria, VA) recently held a member recruitment event that increased membership by over 21 percent in one week.

Executive Director Holly Dougherty explains how the dramatic growth happened.

Strategic Partnership — "We hired consulting firm My Chamber Connection to plan the event and motivate members. Our members responded positively to a fresh voice with a new approach to recruitment."

Recruiter Training — "Even the most dedicated members need training on how to share the chamber story and the benefits of membership. The event was kicked off by revealing the benefits that sell, and the way to sell them."

Friendly Competition — "In the past we tried to encourage members to recruit by offering prizes. It didn't work. This event featured friendly competition where members were in teams and worked together to out-recruit the other teams. Business people are naturally competitive and having bragging rights and improving the chamber was enough of an incentive."

New Approach — "It is common for recruitment campaigns to go on for months and lose momentum. Members want to make a difference with as little time investment as possible. Keeping the contest to one week allowed everyone to focus their energy and produce a great result."

Source: Holly Dougherty, Executive Director, Mount Vernon-Lee Chamber of Commerce, Alexandria, VA.
E-mail: hollydougherty@mtvernon-leechamber.org

Use Paid Advertising to Recruit New Members

Finding improved methods to recruit new members is imperative to every member-based organization. One method to consider is using paid advertisements to reach new member prospects.

Staff with the Chamber of Commerce of Sandusky County (Fremont, OH) first utilized paid advertising during their 60-day membership campaign in 2006, says Holly Stacy, president and CEO.

After creating a budget of roughly $600, Stacy says, she and fellow staff members decided to purchase ads in the business section of the local paper and radio spots. Produced by the radio station, the 30- and 60-second spots used a script based on input from the chamber staff and recorded using existing radio talent.

Stacy and her staff negotiated incentives from the radio station to use in their membership campaign: "If I bought $400 worth of radio spots for my campaign, they gave me four $100 coupons that we could use as prize incentives for drawings for the referring members and for the new members."

She notes that without these incentives, she may not have chosen that station for her campaign, as she was looking for incentives to use as prizes for members.

Stacy says negotiating the incentive package with the radio station was easy, as the radio station is already marketing to virtually the same audience as the chamber is. Any member who wins a coupon for radio advertising may

then turn into a new client for the station, making it a win-win for all involved.

The money used for these advertising efforts came from the dues generated from the new members joining the chamber.

Stacy and her colleagues at the chamber are busy working on creating another paid advertising campaign.

"The new campaign will be a concentrated effort in four days with volunteer teams," says Stacy. For the campaign, some advertising spots may be different than the previous campaign and may include member testimonials in the radio advertisements.

Stacy says the paid advertising definitely has a positive impact on membership. During the paid advertising drive two years ago, the chamber brought in more than 20 new members.

For the next campaign, they hope to bring in 36 or more new members.

Stacy says their motivation for incorporating paid advertisements into the chamber's outreach efforts was to provide prospective members with information from various angles and keep the chamber's name fresh in the minds of community members.

"Members need to hear the information from more than one angle," Stacy says. "Just radio or just newspaper ads alone won't work."

Source: Holly M. Stacy, CEO/President, Chamber of Commerce of Sandusky County, Fremont, OH. E-mail: ceo@scchamber.org

Membership Management Essentials for Chambers of Commerce

Use Popular YouTube Site to Promote Your Cause

Online options for marketing your membership continue to grow. For instance, the popular online video-sharing site, YouTube, now boasts a nonprofit channel where associations, organizations and nonprofits can get more exposure for planned events and offerings.

Staff with The Greater Omaha Chamber of Commerce (Omaha, NE) have posted several videos and photo streams on YouTube. Costs were minimal, since the chamber and its economic development arm, the Greater Omaha Economic Development Partnership, had already produced the videos to promote Omaha for other projects.

Uploading the videos to YouTube "was a way for more eyes to see each project," says RuthAnn Manley, the chamber's director of communications.

In the first 12 months on the website, the video, "This Is Omaha," received nearly 6,000 hits; a photo stream set to music titled, "Omaha O! Public Art Project," received more than 2,000 views; and "Omaha O! Greater Omaha Chamber of Commerce," a video featuring the mayor and other area officials speaking about the Omaha experience, brought in some 1,000 hits.

To boost your organization's visibility with YouTube, try these simple steps:

- Go to www.youtube.com, hit "Signup" and answer questions to create a profile about your organization.

- Once logged in, click the "Upload" button at top right of YouTube's home page. This takes you to a form to describe your project. Complete the form for video upload including title, description, video category (select "Nonprofit & Activism"), tags (keywords to identify your video), broadcast options, date/map options and sharing options.

- To attach the video, browse and select your already-created video or photo stream from your computer and hit "Upload a video" button. Videos must be no more than 10 minutes and no larger than 24 MB.

Source: RuthAnn Manley, Director of Communications, Greater Omaha Chamber of Commerce, Omaha, NE.
E-mail: rmanley@omahachamber.org

Give Members a Reason to Belong

Persons looking for motivation to join the Mooresville-South Iredell Chamber of Commerce (Mooresville, NC) don't have to look far. The chamber's website posts 10 reasons why membership with the chamber is so important:

1. **New business contacts:** Networking and new business contacts help your business grow. With nearly 1,100 members representing thousands of area employees, the chamber speaks with a strong voice for our business community.
2. **Credibility:** Credibility to make a statement that you are committed to the future of Iredell County.
3. **Leadership development:** Learning opportunities/ professional development to help you run a smarter, more profitable business.
4. **Community commitment:** Promote the community to help residents enjoy greater opportunities.
5. **Referrals:** Referrals and sales opportunities to deliver return on your investment.
6. **Publicity and exposure:** Publicity and heightened name recognition, so customers know who you are.
7. **Marketing and advertising:** Targeted and affordable advertising to help your business effectively grow on any budget.
8. **A healthy local environment:** Create a strong local economy to keep our business momentum moving forward.
9. **Gain a voice in the government:** The chamber is your representative on the local, regional, state and national level. Your voice is heard on vital regulatory, legislative and educational issues affecting your business.
10. **Activities:** Getting involved in the many activities the chamber has to offer leads to valuable relationships and gratification in serving the community.

Source: Karen Shore, President/CEO, Mooresville-South Iredell Chamber of Commerce, Mooresville, NC.
E-mail: kas@mooresvillenc.org

Offer Incentives to Join Beyond the Typical Top 10

While Top 10 lists catch attention, the Pasadena Chamber of Commerce (Pasadena, CA) more than doubles that by giving 21 reasons to join, which is helping to spur membership growth, says Paul Little, chamber president and CEO of the 1,500-member organization.

"In putting together our 21 reasons," Little says, "we boiled the benefits of joining down to bullet points and added some items that are unique to our chamber. We also ranked the items in a way that seem to be most important to our members and potential members."

Source: Paul Little, President and CEO, Pasadena Chamber of Commerce, Pasadena, CA. Phone (626) 795-3355. E-mail: Paul@pasadena-chamber.org.

The Pasadena Chamber of Commerce (Pasadena, CA) website features this list of 21 reasons to join.

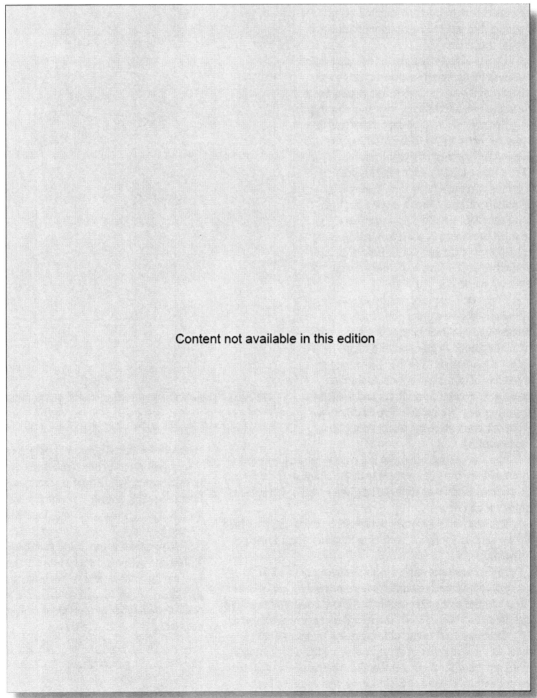

Content not available in this edition

Membership Management Essentials for Chambers of Commerce.
Edited by Scott C. Stevenson.
© 2012 Stevenson, Inc. Published 2012 by Stevenson, Inc.

Membership Management Essentials for Chambers of Commerce

It's important to have procedures in place aimed at nurturing relationships with your newest chamber members. Besides making them fully aware of what's available to them as members, it's important to get a more complete understanding of what matters most to them. What you do during that first year of membership can help to improve member retention rates during the years that follow.

Member Orientation Highlights Benefits, Overall Value

Do all you can to engage and interact with new members to get them excited about membership and talking it up with other potential members.

One proven technique for doing so is to host a dynamic member orientation to welcome newcomers and give them valuable information on maximizing their membership.

Member orientations are important first steps for newcomers to the Minneapolis Regional Chamber of Commerce (Minneapolis, MN), says Lisa Myhre, director of membership development. Typically offered twice a month, the hour-long orientations allow new members to meet the chamber president, member relations coordinator, public policy director and other staff, as well as other new and existing members.

"We begin the program by allowing attendees to give a quick introduction of themselves and their companies along with what they hope to gain through membership," Myhre says. "We then move into an overview of our organization, including programs, events, committees and marketing opportunities. We include live testimonials from our committee members throughout the program."

New members receive an informational packet detailing how they can get involved with the chamber, plus a Next Steps form (shown at above) that gives specific examples of how they can do so.

Orientations take place at various locations and are paid for by various sponsors, including Starbucks and Principal Financial.

Myhre says she strives to limit attendees to 15 to 20 persons to help each attendee have a rewarding experience: "The smaller size helps people feel more comfortable asking questions and we, as staff, can spend more time with them."

Chamber staff invite new members to orientation meetings in a number of ways, including handwritten notes thanking them for their membership, welcome e-mails that go out within 24 hours of joining, as well as notes in the

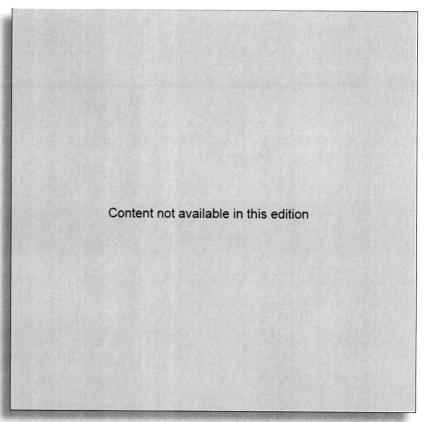

Content not available in this edition

Newcomers complete this "next steps" form at orientation to encourage them to maximize membership with the Minneapolis Regional Chamber of Commerce (Minneapolis, MN).

chamber's e-newsletters and online calendar.

Orientations prove doubly rewarding as they educate new members while helping the chamber retain them over time, she says, noting: "We have a much higher success rate with retaining members who have attended an orientation meeting.

"Our chamber has 1,800 members and provides more than 150 events per year," says Myhre. "These meetings help members navigate through what we have to offer them, and also give them a good idea of what events and programs to attend to reach certain types of individuals and/or companies to do business with."

Source: Lisa Myhre, Director of Membership Development, Minneapolis Regional Chamber of Commerce, Minneapolis, MN. E-mail: lmyhre@minneapolischamber.org

Membership Certificates: Signed, Sealed and Framed

The Glenpool Chamber of Commerce (Glenpool, OK) awards each new member a certificate of membership. The 8 1/2 X 11-inch framed certificate is signed by the chamber's president. Bearing a gold seal, the certificate is meant to show that the recipient is an official member in good standing with the local chamber.

Chamber officials have presented nearly 145 members certificates to date.

Once awarded the certificate — which is presented at a chamber luncheon — the chamber member has the opportunity to talk about his/her business to members in attendance. A local newspaper reporter is on hand to take photos of the member receiving the award and write an article about the member and his/her business for the local paper.

Tying the awarding of the certificate with the opportunity for the member to talk about his/her business to fellow members as well as getting newspaper coverage makes this a wonderful opportunity for members to get awareness in the community about their business venture while offering recognition for the chamber's efforts, says Carol Campbell, executive director.

"The members really like this, as it gives them an extra chance to promote their business, and the certificate acts as a point of recognition at their business," Campbell says.

Even if your membership is not part of a chamber, you may consider awarding members with a certificate of membership to honor and recognize each member as being an integral part of your organization.

Source: Carol Campbell, Executive Director, Glenpool Chamber of Commerce, Glenpool, OK. E-mail: GlenpoolChamber@yahoo.com

Create Casual Environment for Orienting Members

Creating an atmosphere that encourages interaction with your staff in an intimate, comfortable setting will help your organization establish strong relationships with your newest members.

Staff with the Sedona Chamber of Commerce (Sedona, AZ) began holding new member orientations earlier this year. Jennifer Wesselhoff, president/CEO, shares tips for creating an intimate and casual environment for orientations:

- **Keep number of attendees relatively small.** Wesselhoff says they limit orientations to 15-20 members.

- **Allow current members to attend.** Some of the chamber's current members have attended the last two orientation meetings to learn about new programs and services.

- **Invite board members.** Wesselhoff invites one or two board members to orientations to speak to new members, which she says helps them understand the chamber leadership.

- **Create handouts, but keep the presentation personal.** "While we do hand out a packet to each attendee detailing the presentations being made," she says, "all of the information is articulated by chamber staff and board members."

- **Give new members a chance to introduce themselves.** At the beginning of the chamber's event, Wesselhoff says, members have the chance to introduce themselves to the group and network.

- **Include a question-and-answer session.** "After the presentations are made, we open up the discussion for questions from our members," Wesselhoff says. "They always have a lot of questions for us."

- **Have your staff remain available after the orientation is over.** Wesselhoff says members often approach the chamber's staff immediately after the orientation with additional questions or ideas for new programs.

Source: Jennifer Wesselhoff, President/CEO, Sedona Chamber of Commerce, Sedona, AZ.

Ice Breakers Quickly Turn Acquaintances Into Friends

When attending a group meeting for the first time, new members can often feel like outsiders as other members stay in their familiar groups.

That's where ice breakers can help.

Staff with the Greater Nashua Chamber of Commerce (Nashua, NH) regularly use ice breakers at membership events, adding incentive and fun by giving participants the chance to win prizes.

"As staff members and ambassadors, we tend to know most of the people attending our events and are comfortable moving from group to group, because we're not approaching strangers," says Tracy Hatch, director of membership. "It can be easy to forget that some of our members know very few people and can feel shy about walking up to a group of people all laughing and talking together as if they've know each other for years."

Hatch says that several years ago, chamber ambassadors devised a new approach to breaking that clique feeling — adding easy-to-do ice breakers. The conversation starters make it easier for members to approach people they might not know.

Hatch shares ice breaker ideas to help new members feel comfortable and fit in:

- **Tie ice breaker in with event venue.** For example, when hosting an event at a local bath remodeling store, attendees were charged with finding five members who had recently remodeled their bathrooms. For an event at a local hotel featuring a saltwater pool, attendees had to find five members who had been in a saltwater pool before.
- **Create an ice breaker that forges relationships with leadership.** When the chamber elected ambassadors, the all-member ice breaker was to find five ambassadors.

Content not available in this edition

- **Ensure new members successfully integrate with group as a whole.** Use the Find-five-new-members ice breaker to encourage interaction with new members and force existing members to seek out fresh faces in the crowd.

Source: Tracy Hatch, Director of Membership, Greater Nashua Chamber of Commerce, Nashua, NH. E-mail: thatch@ nashuachamber.com

Organizers of member events for the Greater Nashua Chamber of Commerce (Nashua, NH) use simple forms such as this to promote ice breakers that get members mingling and offer members the chance to win prizes.

Give Specific Directions on How to Maximize Membership

Do all you can to spotlight member benefits for prospective and current members.

For inspiration, look to the website for the Greater Nashua Chamber of Commerce (Nashua, NH), where people simply click "Join the Chamber," then "10 Easy Steps."

"It's so important for new members to get active in the chamber early in their membership," says Tracy Hatch, director of membership. "They meet people, begin to form relationships with other chamber members and our staff, and can more easily see that their membership is a true investment for their business, not just an expense. Then when renewal comes around, they've had a positive experience that makes them much more likely to remain members."

The chamber's 10 online steps are:

1. Download and complete the membership application.
2. Check calendar of events page and sign up for a member orientation.
3. Get your business on the chamber's website.
4. Sign up for weekly member briefings that include calendar of events and information on the work of the chamber.
5. Attend a membership orientation and meet over a dozen other new members.
6. Visit the chamber office and introduce yourself to the staff. The chamber encourages staff to promote member businesses. By helping the staff members learn more about your business, they can offer better referrals.
7. Request a membership list. New members receive the latest copy of the chamber's membership at orientation.
8. Request an ambassador. Ambassadors meet members at networking events and help them meet new people and make business contacts.
9. Attend a Business After Hours networking event to meet new people and make valuable business contacts.
10. Stay involved. Chamber staff encourage new members to stay involved in what the organization is doing which will help their business succeed.

Breakfast Orientation Meetings Provide More than Eggs

New members of the Kirkwood-Des Peres Area Chamber of Commerce (Kirkwood, MO) enjoy information-packed orientation sessions over a casual weekday breakfast.

"Enjoying a meal together during a morning orientation helps to keep our new members informed on how they can make the most of their chamber investment," says Gina March, vice president of marketing for the chamber. "The more goods and services they can use to build their businesses, the more likely they are to feel a connection to us, and that affinity builds."

The chamber hosts the breakfast events three to four times a year.

"These breakfast events benefit members by providing information on what services and products the chamber offers," March says. "They also get to meet each staff person (who explains what she does), as well as all the ambassadors and board members. There is also lots of networking before and after the event. And, of course, free breakfast. In the last two years, our attendance has climbed dramatically from 40 in September 2007 to 110 by June 2009. Each event in between was better attended than the one before."

March shares four tips for organizing a successful breakfast orientation for members:

❑ Invite businesses that do not have early morning business hours to host the event. For example, she says, "Our local Red Robin Gourmet Burgers (which only serves lunch and dinner fare) has been thrilled to create a breakfast buffet for members attending the event."

❑ Get members personally involved in the process to invite newcomers to the event. Include existing members on your invitation list and get the word out in print and electronic means. "New members want to learn all they can about getting involved," she says, "and veteran members want to network with new members."

❑ Invite a business to be the host sponsor. In the chamber's case, this means getting a two-minute infomercial and having a booth at the event. Sponsors pay $300 to host the event and receive other benefits, such as having their company's logo on fax/e-mail blasts and posted on the member orientation website.

❑ Don't create handouts for every event and service you offer. "It is a lot of copying and folder stuffing that is mostly useless," March says. "We learned the hard way by picking up all the folders people left behind or didn't take. Now we ask all members to get out their business card and hold it up for everyone to see. Then we tell them to hang on to their card and write every question, request or additional info they want on the back of it. We pick them up at the end of the event and follow up with each one of them."

Source: Gina March, Vice President of Marketing, Kirkwood-Des Peres Area Chamber of Commerce, Kirkwood, MO. E-mail: gina@thechamber.us

Content not available in this edition

Business Fair Allows New Members to Show Their Stuff

How can organizations demonstrate value to new members, especially when economic conditions make membership dues harder to justify?

Tailor events to their needs, says Nicole Kelliher, marketing coordinator of the Lower Bucks County Chamber of Commerce (Fairless Hills, PA.) Kelliher's organization did so with its New Member Business Fair. Held on chamber premises, the event gave businesses that had joined the chamber within a certain time frame the opportunity to showcase their services and products for the entire membership.

The event featured 21 new businesses and drew some 80 chamber members. Registration fees ran $25 for all eligible members.

Having easily met goals of participating vendors and registration revenue, Kelliher counts the event as a solid success. "Members found it a fantastic networking opportunity and valued the opportunity to display their products. Some even suggested extending it into a third hour next time," she says.

Because of this positive reception, Kelliher and her chamber colleagues are already planning another fair.

Source: Nicole Kelliher, Marketing Coordinator, Lower Bucks County Chamber of Commerce, Fairless Hills, PA. E-mail: Nkelliher@lbccc.org

Help Members Energize the Expo Experience

To ensure participants got the most out of the New Member Business Fair, officials at the Lower Bucks County Chamber of Commerce (Fairless Hills, PA) e-mailed participants tips drawn from a recent chamber seminar entitled "Experience Expo Marketing That Really Works."

Here are some of the pointers participating businesses received prior to participating in the business fair:

❑ The best way to have a successful experience at any expo-type event is to leverage your investment.

❑ Develop a tradeshow plan to determine what you want from the event. Write it down and share it with those who will be working the event.

❑ Create a buzz — Announce on your website that you will be participating in the event, send invitations to your customers and potential customers who are fellow chamber members.

❑ Develop a hook — Provide giveaway promotional items, offer a door prize, create special offers (special price on show items or special rates if you book an appointment today).

❑ Plan a display that stands out — Incorporate your company logo, colors and image to attract the kind of attention that you want.

❑ A tablecloth can really dress up your table and allow you to store things under the table unseen.

❑ Offer a door prize by collecting business cards and pulling the lucky winner. This ensures that you will have the contact information of the event attendees so you can follow up with them after the event.

❑ Follow-up — Contact every qualified lead after the event with thank-you notes and requests for face-to-face meetings.

❑ Arrive early and have your booth set up in plenty of time so you don't feel rushed.

❑ Set up quickly and quietly and store your boxes out of sight.

❑ Maintain an orderly space. Do not leave food or beverages lying around.

❑ Have quality conversations with everyone who enters your booth. You never know if that person will become your customer or refer you to someone else.

❑ Relax, smile and have fun!

Membership Management Essentials for Chambers of Commerce

E-Decal Benefits Member Organization, Members

Chambers of commerce have long provided members with chamber identification for promotional purposes. The Greater Wilmington Chamber of Commerce (Wilmington, NC) takes that idea a step further by offering an e-decal — a specially designed version of the standard chamber logo — that members may use on their websites and in communications supporting electronic graphics.

"Our new members always get a sticker to put on their door or window," says Scott Czechlewski, director of communications. "This is just a way to put that same logo on a website or e-mail."

The e-decal is available free to all member organizations. Interested persons simply fill out an online user agreement stipulating that they will not change or alter the logo. They then receive the logo in electronic format in three sizes in a JPEG image file format.

The e-decal is explained in member orientations, and Czechlewski estimates that one-fourth to one-third of all new members request it.

"It's particularly popular with smaller businesses or businesses that are new to the area," he says. "It's a way to show real involvement with the community. It also leverages the reputation and credibility of a well-respected organization seen to be the voice of the business community."

And the benefit to the chamber? "It's free publicity," Czechlewski says simply. The inexpensive member benefit "publicizes the services we offer to members and shows the strength we have in the community."

Source: Scott Czechlewski, Director of Communications, Greater Wilmington Chamber of Commerce, Wilmington, NC. E-mail: czechlewski@wilmingtonchamber.org

New Member Receptions Offer Networking, Acclimation

A new member reception is the ideal way to warmly receive new members and integrate them into your membership.

At the Rochester Area Chamber of Commerce (Rochester, MN), new member receptions take place every other month. On average, 50 to 60 new members attend the receptions that launch them into the growing 1,300 member totals.

Judy Braatz, membership development director, offers tips for implementing successful new member receptions:

- Ask current members to host and offer new members a free luncheon with ample opportunity to network.

- Allow new members to attend the event one time after joining, but offer them plenty of time — such as six months — in which to do so. By offering a new member reception every other month, new members of the Rochester chamber can select the date that works best for them.

- Formally invite new members by mailed invitation.

- Have the president and pertinent staff introduce themselves to new members and answer questions at the event.

- Alert new members prior to the event that they will have an opportunity to introduce themselves in front of guests. This allows them to prepare and pare down their introduction to the allotted timeframe. At the new member receptions held by the Rochester Area Chamber of Commerce, members are asked to give a one-minute introductory speech.

- Encourage new members to bring literature about their business to share. Rochester Chamber events include a display table where new members can put business cards and/or brochures.

- Place volunteers throughout the event to facilitate introductions and conversation among new members.

- Consider offering door prizes with winners being announced at the end of the event to ensure that new members stay for the entire event.

Source: Judy Braatz, Membership Development Director, Rochester Area Chamber of Commerce, Rochester, MN. E-mail: JBraatz@RochesterMNChamber.com

Membership Management Essentials for Chambers of Commerce

RENEWAL AND RETENTION EFFORTS

Membership renewal is a science. It's important to have a well thought-out system of renewal procedures in place as you make every effort to retain members from year to year. Your series of renewal attempts may include a variety of techniques, as well — letters, phone calls, e-mails and face-to-face visits — all intended to ensure that the highest number of members choose to continue their association with your chamber.

Drive Members to Renew

Increased competition for members' attention, time and money makes renewal as challenging as ever. Having good procedures in place is important, but a truly effective renewal program takes more than that.

Melody Jordan-Carr, senior director of member relations for ASAE, and Jennifer St. John, a membership representative with 10 years of experience with the Los Angeles Chamber of Commerce, explain what really drives members to renew:

Incentivize the right behavior — Offering a 60 to 90 day grace period after membership has expired is common practice, but it also might encourage members to renew later than they otherwise would. Reward those who pay on time. The Los Angeles Chamber of Commerce gives a 10 percent discount to members who renew on or before the due date. The chamber has seen an increase in early member renewals since this was instituted.

Know your members' fiscal years — Contact members when they are most likely to spend money, often at the beginning of their fiscal year.

Track members' staff — Staff turnover at member organizations can make or break renewal. Make sure to connect with new staff and get them involved right away.

Make payment easy — Consider providing payment plan options instead of requiring all of the money up front. Also, allow numerous ways to pay: online, snail mail and over the phone.

Approach renewal as a holistic process — Don't wait for the renewal cycle to begin before reaching out to members. Engage them throughout the year and make sure they experience value. Value is as much about member perception as it is about organizational offerings. Know the reasons a member joined and connect them with the appropriate services, so their expectations are met.

Sources: Melody Jordan-Carr, Senior Director, Member Relations, ASAE, Washington, D.C.
E-mail: mcarr@asaecenter.org
Jennifer St. John, Membership Representative, Los Angeles Chamber of Commerce, Los Angeles, CA.
E-mail: jstjohn@lachamber.com

Encourage Members to Renew Early With Incentives

Create a program to provide members with worthwhile incentives for early renewal.

Staff with The Greater Brandon Chamber of Commerce (Brandon, FL) started their renewal rewards program in 2006 to reward members who paid dues prior to their anniversary date, says Janet Noah, director, member services.

The program began after an area newspaper and chamber member offered $100 vouchers good toward any new ad purchased in any of its publications for chamber members who renewed early.

The rewards program revolves around chamber members donating prizes as incentive to renew before the anniversary date, says Noah. Initially, she reached out to a variety of members to see if they would be interested in participating in this program. Once a few members came on board, other members began to inquire about participating.

Rewards range from a mail center coupon, free meal, free ads in chamber and other publications and free flyer placements, as well as the chance to win member-donated prizes. Members who donate prizes are listed in the cham-

ber's monthly newsletter and on its website.

Current members are reminded about the renewal rewards in two ways, a member renewal page on the chamber's website and on the invoices they receive prior to their renewal date. The chamber is not currently tracking how many members renewed early because of this program.

When developing a renewal rewards program, Noah advises, start simply. Consider sending a mass mailing to tell members about the program and ask them to donate prizes. While prizes need not be extravagant, strive to gather a variety of prizes to appeal to more of your members.

Once you have the donated prizes in place, look for ways to publicize this program to members and get them excited about the possibility of winning rewards. Allow members to renew online, by mail, at events and in person at your office.

Finally, remember to market this prize incentive to people considering becoming members of your organization.

Source: Janet Noah, Director, Member Services, The Greater Brandon Chamber of Commerce, Brandon, FL.
E-mail: jnoah@brandonchamber.com

Membership Management Essentials for Chambers of Commerce

Honesty and Frequency Boost Membership Numbers

Success for one organization started with a 23 percent drop in membership numbers.

"Our success began with finding our true number," Bonnie Grady, currently president/CEO at the Chamber of Commerce of the Mid-Ohio Valley (Parkersburg, WV), says of her prior position at Carroll County Chamber of Commerce (Westminster, MD).

"When I began (at the Carroll County Chamber), I was told there were 'around 600' active members," Grady says. "What I found was a lot of dead wood on the books: members who had not renewed, were not active and — in some cases — not even in business anymore. We cleaned up the membership records and, when it all shook out, the true number was 463 (23 percent less than 600). At its highest point over the next six years, it would top out at 669," a 44 percent increase over the true number.

To boost membership, Grady and her staff focused on maximizing the number of touches each member received by revamping their ambassadors program.

"Each month, ambassadors drew names from the membership list and then reached out to those members by phone, personal letter, e-mail or in person before their next committee meeting," she says. "Ambassadors could also earn points for arranging to meet a new member at a breakfast or luncheon and introducing their new friend to other members, attending chamber events, submitting new member leads and even for picking up the bagels for the monthly chamber orientation program."

Point leaders were named Ambassador of the Month and Ambassador of the Year.

Ultimately, says Grady, success is all about meeting members' needs. "Whether at a chamber meeting or in line at the grocery store, we all tried to develop opportunities to talk with our members, hear their needs and find ways to address those needs."

Source: Bonnie Grady, President/CEO, Chamber of Commerce of the Mid-Ohio Valley, Parkersburg, WV.
E-mail: bgrady@movchamber.org

Retention Starts Before Day One

During her tenure at a prior chamber of commerce, Bonnie Grady, currently president/CEO at the Chamber of Commerce of the Mid-Ohio Valley (Parkersburg, WV), helped increase membership by 44 percent and enjoyed a 96 percent retention rate.

The membership expert says retention is just as important as recruitment.

"The most important thing to remember is that retention starts before Day One," she says. "Before you embark on a membership campaign, make that first call or send that first e-mail, you have to know what it is you're selling. Your membership team must understand the value of membership: What are the benefits? How do they work? What does each benefit mean to each member?"

Grady cites the four most critical aspects of recruiting new members — and retaining members — as:

1. **Signaling value** — Educate prospective members on why they should belong; quantify it, if you can.
2. **Offering exceptional customer service.**
3. **Staying on top of disengaged members** — Identify them, talk to them, bring them back in.
4. **Keeping your numbers clean** — Know your true membership numbers.

Consider Staff Position Dedicated to Renewals

If your membership renewal tactics are falling short, look for some fresh tactics.

The Greater Casa Grande Chamber of Commerce (Casa Grande, AZ) added a full-time membership sales representative about four years ago, says Helen Neuharth, president/CEO.

"Growth in our business community was rapid, and there was simply no one on staff who had the time to dedicate to membership recruitment and retention that was necessary to grow the chamber," Neuharth says. "The rep begins to contact businesses who are 45 days overdue (and again at 90 days overdue), reviewing membership benefits and talking to them about the reasons they may be considering not renewing.

"The rep contacts the business, offers to drive to the business and pick up the check, or change the dues payment from annual to six-month renewal," she says.

As motivation, Neuharth says the sales rep receives 10 percent commission on renewals for overdue memberships that are paid prior to being placed on the board agenda to be dropped.

The combination of having a dedicated staff person devoted to member retention and offering flexible options to renewing members "has proven to be a very effective means of generating renewal revenue," Neuharth says, "as the person-to-person contact with the members and listening to their concerns and offering to make their decision to renew more financially feasible for them, is meaningful to many chamber members."

Source: Helen Neuharth, President/CEO, Greater Casa Grande Chamber of Commerce, Casa Grande, AZ.
E-mail: president@casagrandechamber.org

Membership Management Essentials for Chambers of Commerce

Member Orientations Increase Involvement, Retain Membership

When should an organization begin working to retain new members? From the very beginning, says Jane Anderson, vice president of member services, Asheville Area Chamber of Commerce (Asheville, NC).

"We've always felt it's critical to get members engaged as quickly as possible," Anderson says. "That's why we see new member orientations as such an essential part of our retention strategy."

"Starting new members off with a few satisfying interactions can make all the difference."

The Asheville chamber hosts a new member orientation every month. Regularly drawing 20 to 45 participants, these popular meetings reach an estimated 80 percent of all new members.

As impressive as the figures for new member orientations may be, Anderson emphasizes that chamber staff still track orientation attendance and place follow-up calls to members who miss their most immediate meeting. She notes that staff has even been known to hold one-on-one orientations for members who face conflicts that make attending regularly scheduled events impossible.

The half-day program begins with a sponsored breakfast and introductory welcome from the chamber's president. New members are invited to introduce themselves and then present 30-second commercials for their businesses. The morning's agenda also includes a time for chamber departments to describe their services, and an informal, brief PowerPoint presentation.

Because chamber officials feel it is important for new members to hear first-hand accounts of the chamber's services, Anderson says, they try to include a few current members in every orientation. They also incorporate elements of outreach and recruiting by encouraging anyone considering chamber membership to attend an orientation.

Asked what newcomers gain from these new member orientations, Anderson highlights four key areas:

❑ **Physical facilities**. Members become familiar with the chamber facilities — board room, meeting rooms, etc. — that are available to them.

❑ **Resources**. Members are introduced to both standard chamber services as well as the functions that are unique to the Asheville chamber.

❑ **Relationships**. Members begin the process of putting faces to names and developing relationships with each other and staff.

❑ **Fun**. "If nothing else, they walk away having had a good time," says Anderson. "It sounds so simple, but starting new members off with a few satisfying interactions can make all the difference."

Source: Jane Anderson, Vice President of Member Services, Asheville Area Chamber of Commerce, Asheville, NC.
E-mail: Janderson@ashevillechamber.org

To Attract New Recruits, Serve Existing Members Well

Bonnie Grady, President/CEO, Chamber of Commerce of the Mid-Ohio Valley (Parkersburg, WV), says membership organizations that put recruitment as the No. 1 priority should consider putting retention there instead.

Unless you are a new organization, you have members already, Grady says. Focus first on serving them well in order to make membership look attractive to prospective members. "If you're doing a good job of making your members feel valued, and you promote those achievements," she says, "others will notice and want to be part of your organization."

Here are a few ways Grady says work to keep existing members happy:

✓ **Create and promote programs that cause prospective members to seek you out.** "You have to have specific benefits that speak to prospective members. Then you can begin to promote those benefits. For example, we've launched a new program called the Nonprofit Executives' Roundtable. Nonprofit organizations — both members and nonmembers — are invited to a 90-minute session where they share news of upcoming projects and events, identify resources, address concerns and share best practices. Since nonprofit boards are made up of local business reps, we're casting a wide net. We expect to see more local nonprofits joining the chamber as a result of this new initiative."

✓ **Create payoffs for your volunteers.** "Our points-based rewards system in my former chamber helped our ambassadors set their own goals and achieve them. We've started a similar program at the MOV Chamber and we call the volunteers Chamber Champions. Now the membership development committee has asked if they can have a points system, too!"

✓ **Listen, listen and listen.** "The simplest conversation can provide clues to what prospective members fear the most, what they want more than anything else and what they are willing to do to get it."

Source: Bonnie Grady, President/CEO, Chamber of Commerce of the Mid-Ohio Valley, Parkersburg, WV.
E-mail: bgrady@movchamber.org

Membership Management Essentials for Chambers of Commerce

Answer One Crucial Question To Key In to Your Members

Asking, "What keeps my members awake at night?" is the most critical tool for any membership professional, says Bonnie Grady, president/CEO, Chamber of Commerce of the Mid-Ohio Valley (Parkersburg, WV). "Whether at a chamber meeting or in line at the grocery store," Grady says, "we try to develop opportunities to talk with our members, hear their needs and find ways to address them."

Grady cites another key tool to successful membership management: "the courage to try new things, introduce new programs and kill off old ones if they're not working." While such decisions aren't always popular, she says, they do open the door for growth and necessary change.

Source: Bonnie Grady, President/CEO, Chamber of Commerce of the Mid-Ohio Valley, Parkersburg, WV. E-mail: bgrady@movchamber.org

To Grow Interest, Limit Top Membership Categories

Every parent knows the surest way to interest a child in something is to tell the child it is off limits. Some things never change. The more people are told they can't have something, the more they want it.

Officials at the Bellevue Chamber of Commerce (Bellevue, WA) leverage a similar principle in restricting access to their top two membership packages.

Offering exclusive benefits and privileges such as access to special events and unique recognition opportunities, the chamber's Premier membership package and Executive membership package are each limited to 10 percent of total chamber membership.

But while membership is intentionally restricted, Ellen Asbell, who oversees membership and marketing, says no business is rejected out of hand. "If anyone wants to look at that level, it's always open for discussion."

Source: Ellen Asbell, Membership & Marketing, Bellevue Chamber of Commerce, Bellevue, WA.

Keeping Score Helps Build A Winning Ambassador Team

A little healthy competition never hurt anyone — and sometimes it can really help. Just ask Leslee Fritz, marketing opportunities account manager at the Grand Rapids Area Chamber of Commerce (Grand Rapids, MI), where a point scale creates some fun competition and keeps member ambassadors on track with their responsibilities.

Any employee of a member business can apply to be a part of the Ambassador Club. Ambassadors are charged with retaining the chamber's membership through mentorship and involvement. Here's how it works:

A point value is assigned to each ambassador opportunity (e.g., ribbon-cutting ceremonies garner 10 points; personal visits with current chamber members, 25 points; recruiting a new member, 100 points). Ambassadors, who track and report their points on a monthly basis, are required to earn a minimum of 200 points each month.

Ambassadors who earn the most points receive special recognition. Each month, the ambassador with the highest point total is featured in the chamber's newsletter and on the website. The ambassador with the highest total points for the year receives a special award.

Keep competitions simple and fun, Fritz says. "Remember the primary focus and set goals for the group." She says the point system helps the chamber do that for its ambassadors, keeping them focused on their own success, as well as that of the chamber.

Source: Leslee Fritz, Marketing Opportunities Account Manager, Grand Rapids Area Chamber of Commerce, Grand Rapids, MI. E-mail: fritzl@grandrapids.org

Group Buying Electrifies Chamber Membership

While at the Carroll County Chamber of Commerce (Westminster, MD), Bonnie Grady helped boost membership by 44 percent and enjoyed a 96 percent retention rate.

Grady is currently president/CEO for the Chamber of Commerce of the Mid-Ohio Valley (Parkersburg, WV). At the Carroll County Chamber in early 2004, she says, "We stumbled onto the idea of group buying." Upon learning that another Maryland Chamber was bringing members together to negotiate for reduced electricity rates in the newly deregulated marketplace, Grady and her colleagues contracted with the consultant who was managing the other Chamber's buying program to do the same for the Carroll County Chamber.

In the first round, she says, the new program brought in 112 new members and collectively saved the group over $1.5 million.

Grady says the program helped some members cut electric bills by more than 40 percent. "I'll never forget how I felt when a member came to me with tears in her eyes and said, 'If it hadn't been for the Chamber starting that program, I would have had to close my doors.' It's not about the numbers or the revenue; it's about responding to our members' needs."

Source: Bonnie Grady, President/CEO, Chamber of Commerce of the Mid-Ohio Valley, Parkersburg, WV. E-mail: bgrady@movchamber.org

Membership Management Essentials for Chambers of Commerce.
Edited by Scott C. Stevenson.
© 2012 Stevenson, Inc. Published 2012 by Stevenson, Inc.

Membership Management Essentials for Chambers of Commerce

The frequency and ways in which you communicate with Chamber members will impact their level of satisfaction with your organization and their ultimate decision of whether to renew. And emerging social media technologies are allowing even more forms of communication to take place. Explore every available option for staying connected to your chamber members and making new inroads with would-be members.

Boost Member Communication

Are your members well-informed about all the benefits and member-based events available to them? If member feedback — or lack thereof — implies your communication efforts are lacking, consider incorporating new events and resources to better communicate with your valued members.

The Council Grove/Morris County Chamber of Commerce & Tourism (Council Grove, KS) began hearing from some members that there was a lack of communication from the chamber staff, says TinaRae Scott, executive director.

"Roughly 30 percent of our members, mostly younger, said that they were not well-enough informed," Scott says. "These members spoke about this in person with the president of our board, who promised that what they said had not gone unheard and that during her term, she would work to improve communications."

Those improvements include:

❑ **Member E-newsletter** — E-mailed to interested members, the one-page e-newsletter includes upcoming events and photos. Scott says the e-newsletter is still in the early stages, with plans to add additional content.

❑ **Quarterly Breakfasts** — Members who sponsor breakfasts receive agenda time to promote events/businesses. Other presenters may include chamber staff, event chairs and board members. Cost is $5 for chamber members and $6 for non-members, with up to $4 going back to thesponsoring business to cover meal cost. The rest of the money collected goes toward costs to advertise the breakfasts in three local newspapers and cover cost of the door prizes. Door prizes may include a gift certificate to the sponsoring business or general marketing merchandise. The chamber also notifies members of the breakfasts by e-mail and by posting signs on their office bulletin boards and in their office windows.

These responses to members' communications concerns have been very well-received, says Scott, who adds: "We are thrilled with the turnout at the breakfasts and the communication efforts that have come from this request."

Source: TinaRae Scott, Executive Director, Council Grove/Morris County Chamber of Commerce & Tourism, Council Grove, KS. E-mail: chamber@tctelco.net

Use Social Media Effectively to Connect With Members

Are you reaching out to members using all resources available today? If you haven't tapped into social media, you may want to consider jumping on board.

Connecting with its 1,600 members via social media venues has become a priority at the Canton Regional Chamber of Commerce (Canton, OH), according to Jessica Bennett, director of marketing. Prominently displayed at the home Web page and under the Chamber News section of the chamber's website (www.chambernews.org), are large tabs for Facebook, Linkedin, YouTube, an RSS feed and Twitter, which allows members to easily access chamber information from their favorite social media outlets.

"Our chamber promotes a great many events, programs and issues for businesses and business professionals throughout the year, and we promote with a strategic mix of marketing tactics," says Bennett. "Social media allows us to reach our members and community in a simple, affordable and immediate way. With social media, we can reach our audience in the places where they're ready to communicate, ready to absorb. It's less intrusive because the medium is as much a pull as it is a push, when done right."

With more than 1,600 member businesses along with six supporting departments, the chamber reaches thousands of members from the region with each social media notice. In light of this, chamber staff work to not overwhelm members with social media posts by, for example, limiting messages on www.twitter.com (called tweets) to one or two times a week and only offering relevant program and event updates.

Bennett shares tips for communicating with members via social media outlets:

✓ Twitter, Facebook and other social media elements are exceptional listening tools, creating a mainline between an organization and its constituents. Like any good relationship, it needs to be nurtured. Don't be afraid to ask for tips from members/followers.

✓ Be relevant and limit redundancy in social media messages. Your followers have given you permission to communicate; don't abuse it with junk mail or overuse.

✓ Take on what you can handle online, if you overextend, you'll drop the ball. Focus on digital marketing tools you can work with and keep information current as you serve your fans, followers and members.

Source: Jessica Bennett, Director of Marketing, Canton Regional Chamber of Commerce, Canton, OH. E-mail: JessB@cantonchamber.org

Communicate Quickly, Efficiently Through Web Logs

While members would eagerly read the weekly e-newsletter for the Maryland Chamber of Commerce (Annapolis, MD) and chamber officials worked hard to fill it with the latest news, many members wanted more. So chamber officials decided to transition from the editorial model of the newsletter to a more real-time Web log, or blog format.

That was five years ago. Today, that single blog has branched into four separate online Web logs, and chamber members have heartily embraced the role of blogging.

"Blogs are great for associations," says William Burns, the chamber's director of communications. "They naturally build community around a common cause, which is a constant goal of member organizations."

Though chamber officials plan to consolidate several blogs, they will continue to use the online tool to address a range of issues like legislative advocacy, human resources concerns, green and sustainable business, member news and small business tips. This diversity, Burns says, ensures all members find something of interest. He notes that certain topics are noticeably more popular than others, with education-oriented posts among the most heavily viewed. "Things like suggestions for maximizing networking opportunities or pointers on sales and advertising always receive a very enthusiastic response."

Also important is the blog's role in communicating industry-specific news that members often struggle to find elsewhere. "With the blog," Burns says, "we can provide up-to-date information on topics that other media just aren't covering."

Burns cites four key advantages to organizational blogs:

- **Ease of use.** Updating content on a blog is about as easy as it gets, he says, noting that creating and posting an online blog requires far less technical knowledge than preparing a traditional or electronic newsletter.

- **Personality.** "If done right, blogs can develop a persona of their own. This is something we're trying to develop by having multiple staffers post pieces in their own voice."

- **Interaction.** The best blogs also create space for public interaction, says Burns. "They build a powerful community of discussion and action around their content."

- **Informality.** "Blogs are good for translating complex topics into easily digestible portions. In a blog, you can just explain things in normal terms. You don't have to put things the way you would in a press release."

Source: William Burns, Director of Communications, Maryland Chamber of Commerce, Annapolis, MD.
E-mail: wburns@mdchamber.org

Building a Member-pleasing Blog

To help your blog begin the journey from drab to fab, William Burns, director of communications at the Maryland Chamber of Commerce (Annapolis, MD), recommends:

❑ Working to engage members with content. Threads with open-ended questions, online polls and invitations to comment on posts help members become involved and interested.

❑ Incorporating multimedia. "Video demonstrates passion for a subject like nothing else," says Burns. "When kept short and informative, media clips are a great complement to text."

❑ Leveraging local expertise. Featuring tips and suggestions from current members provides information from a reputable local source and reinforces member-to-member relationships.

❑ Starting simple. For first-time bloggers, Burns says to forget presentation and focus on content. "Go to a free service like Wordpress.com or Blogger.com and just start talking about what you know. Incorporating the blog into your site can wait until you have built up your following a bit."

Membership Management Essentials for Chambers of Commerce

Use Software to Coordinate Membership Contact

Gina March, vice president of marketing, Kirkwood-Des Peres Area Chamber of Commerce (Kirkwood, MO), prides herself on offering members a personal approach to membership. With the help of ACT!, a member management software, March has created a two-year system that guarantees the chamber contacts new members a minimum of 18 times.

"The first two or three years is when you're likely to lose a member, and we needed a systematic way to stay in touch with members," March says.

"A chamber member donated the ACT! software to our chamber," she says, adding, "It's so user friendly."

Upon joining, a new member receives a welcome phone call from a staff member and the chamber president and a packet of new member information.

Prompted by the software program, March says that over the course of two years, a new member will be contacted twice by the recruiter, three times by the president of the chamber, four times by one of the 12 chamber ambassadors and nine times by March. She says all of this contact helps to ensure that the member's needs are met.

Members of more than two years are contacted at least seven times a year.

Ambassadors also make courtesy calls to members to get their feedback and to invite them to the next event, says March, noting that this not only makes the member feel valued, but also ensures strong attendance at monthly events.

The software also offers several reporting options such as noting all activities to be completed within a certain date range or to report contacts that have taken place.

"The benefit of creating such reports is to show the board of directors our member contact activity," March says. "This shows we're consciously working on retention."

Putting members' needs first is second nature to March, who owned her own business and was a chamber member before becoming vice president of marketing.

"It was easy for me to recognize what members would like, because I was a member," she says. "My personal passion is to have everyone feel that they are important."

Source: Gina March, Vice President of Marketing, Kirkwood-Des Peres Area Chamber of Commerce, Kirkwood, MO.
E-mail: gina@thechamber.us

Boost Member Contact Through Personalized Mailings

Online services can help personalize and boost mailed correspondence to members.

Susan Pagnozzi, president, Cranston Chamber of Commerce (Cranston, RI), has used the SendOutCards service (www.sendoutcards.com) since early 2007. The service allows persons to choose and fill out greeting cards online, which are sent to designated recipients.

Pagnozzi says the service was introduced to her by Bob Martinelli, president, Emerging Media, LLC (West Greenwich, RI), a chamber member affiliated with SendOutCards.

"I send about five cards a week," says Pagnozzi. "I try to send cards on a monthly basis to renewing members and thank-you cards to anyone who has donated or hosted an event, and I use it faithfully for sympathy messages. There is no limit to the number of cards I can send each month, and there are more than 13,000 cards to choose from."

Cards are printed and mailed the following day unless the sender specifies another date. The service can remind users of important dates such as birthdays or anniversaries. "The people who receive the cards are genuinely excited when they get it," says Pagnozzi. "With e-mail, the days of actually receiving a card in the mail seem to have gone by the wayside. It is so nice to go to the mailbox and get a letter of appreciation, thanks, care, concern or love and not a bill, complaint or additional trash."

Start-up costs range from $99 to $398 plus other account fees. Pagnozzi uses the company's distributor package that includes a onetime fee of $398 and $35 yearly fee.

Martinelli says the service offers two pricing models: Wholesale customers or entrepreneur distributors pay 62 cents per

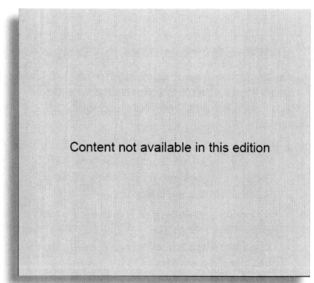

Content not available in this edition

Examples show how member postcards can be personalized.

card plus a first class stamp for a total of $1.03. Retail customers pay 98 cents plus postage, for a total of $1.39.

Existing members can refer the service to others, he adds, noting that when a chamber member signs up as a SendOutCards user, the chamber makes a commission.

Sources: Susan Pagnozzi, President, Cranston Chamber of Commerce, Cranston, RI.
Bob Martinelli Sr., President, Emerging Media, LLC, West Greenwich, RI. E-mail: bob@emergingmedia.biz

Small Membership Staff Can Still Have a Mighty Impact

How do you effectively communicate with and manage your members when you are the only paid employee at your member-based organization?

"I am the only staff member for our chamber," says Diana Lass, executive director, Lincolnwood Chamber (Lincolnwood, IL). "When I took over the position of executive director, we had 85 members; currently, we have roughly 165 members.

"While it is difficult and a constant challenge to maintain close relationships, I have made a commitment to do so. I feel it is what helped in the growth of our membership, so it is important to continue. Relationships are what make our chamber unique."

Lass shares ways she maintains close relationships with her members without the assistance of additional membership staff:

✓ **"My door is always open;** everyone knows they can stop in the office any time they are in the area. All of our members understand I may be out of the office or in a meeting, but the door is always open. Often, if meeting with a prospective member, it affords the opportunity to have a member become a part of the recruiting process.

✓ **"I utilize personal e-mails,** not large blasts, but personal e-mails in the form of a note. It may be a personal invitation to a function, recognition that we haven't seen them for a while or missed them at a function they had registered for and were unable to attend, or just keeping tabs on them in general. While I understand e-mails can be impersonal, if carefully thought out, they can take on the personality of the sender.

✓ **"I visit with members whenever possible.** I do spur-of-the-moment coffees or lunches to keep in touch. By getting to know who our members are and not just what they do in their business, relationships are better established.

✓ **"I create networking opportunities with other member organizations. ...** These groups have become a great resource. Events can be organized with larger attendance as well as administrative support, which for our organization is vital."

While Lass has a structured way to reach members as the solo person on the membership management staff, she does envision a day when she will get help with those efforts.

"If I were able to have additional membership staff, one thing I would like to do is expand the mentoring process for new members," she says. "While we do planned events for new members to meet each other, along with the chamber's board of directors, village administration and village staff, it would be terrific to be able to expand on the idea and offer workshops on how to utilize your membership, take advantage of opportunities and think of the chamber as an extension of your marketing arm."

Source: Diana Lass, Executive Director, Lincolnwood Chamber, Lincolnwood, IL. E-mail: dlass@lincolnwoodchamber.org

Longtime Cable TV Relationship Leads to Online Videos

The Anoka Area Chamber of Commerce (Anoka, MN) has found an innovative way to share members' satisfaction by streaming video testimonials on the chamber's website.

"Nothing works better than having another business owner telling a potential member about their experiences involving the chamber," says Peter Turok, chamber president.

Helping chamber officials put the videos together — at no cost to the chamber —are staff at the local Quad Cities Community Television (QCTV) station.

"We have had a cable TV show featuring the chamber on QCTV for more than 20 years," says Turok of the relationship. "We also have many of their employees involved in the chamber either on committees or as part of the board of directors, so when the need arose, they stepped up." The chamber incurs no fee for the collaboration.

Turok says a committee discussed which members to ask to give testimonials.

"The people that you select should be chamber all-stars," Turok advises, " people you know and who are well-versed on the chamber and its benefits."

Source: Peter Turok, President, Anoka Area Chamber of Commerce, Anoka, MN. E-mail: pete@anokaareachamber.com

President's Journal Connects With Members, Community

If building connections within and beyond your membership is a priority, consider a regular newsletter column, monthly e-mail, Web log or other ongoing correspondence written by one or more of your organization's key players.

For four years, Charlotte Keim, president of the Marietta Area Chamber of Commerce (Marietta, OH), has posted her thoughts, insights, dreams for the chamber, plus shared information and feedback from members and movers and shakers through her President's Journal, a professional blog hosted on the chamber's website (http://mariettachamber.com/3?newstype=2).

The President's Journal features 500- to 600-word essays on topics both occupational and personal. Because the journal is open to the public, its tone differs significantly from other chamber communications, the author notes.

"There is less hard information and more thoughts for reflection and perspective," Keim says. "I try to balance heavy and light, business and non-business, local and regional. To build those personal connections, it helps to have something for everyone."

Recent articles demonstrate this variety of subject matter, ranging from the personal "Thankful for Living in Marietta — My Hometown" to the topical "Marietta Chamber Supports Issue 2 & Marietta School Bond" and the historical "Growing our Economy — A Tale of Marietta from 1921."

For leaders interested in trying such an approach, Keim offers the following tips.

❑ **Don't start if you don't like writing (at least a little).** "If it's a chore for you to write something, it will be a chore for others to read it," she says.

❑ **Don't commit to a strict schedule.** Though Keim aims for bi-weekly postings, she recommends a looser approach for those just beginning.

❑ **Write several entries before posting the first.** "Having a bank of five or six articles will give you some breathing room when things get busy."

❑ **Take notes.** "Most people underestimate how difficult it is to think of ideas when staring at a blank piece of paper," Keim says. "Jotting down interesting stories, statistics and bits of news provides a good source of inspiration."

And a final piece of advice? Keep things positive, advises the chamber president. "Everyone has challenges, and that should be acknowledged," Keim says. "But people are looking for hope and optimism, too. That's what they really respond to."

Source: Charlotte Keim, Marietta Area Chamber of Commerce, Marietta, OH. E-mail: keim@mariettachamber.com

Survey Members in 10 Questions or Less

To maximize the response rate for your next member survey, avoid the temptation to add question after question. Restrict your survey to a maximum of 10 questions and focus your inquiry on areas of high impact and leverage.

A survey from the Alexandria Chamber of Commerce (Alexandria, VA) illustrates how to address a variety of issues with a limited number of questions.

Those questions are summarized here:

1. Please rank the reasons why you joined the chamber: Business development, advocacy, services, access to community leaders, etc.
2. How many chamber events have you attended in (the past year)?
3. If yes, which events? Business After Hours reception, committee meeting, Hot Topics breakfast, professional networking breakfast, etc.
4. How important is the chamber's involvement in the following areas? Local education issues, buy local campaigns, economic development, tourism development, etc.
5. Please rate how the chamber is currently doing in the following areas: overall programs, volunteer leadership, recruitment, communication with members, etc.
6. Please rank the following benefits offered by the chamber: advertising in Who's Who directory, legislative representation, workshops, newsletter.
7. Please rank the most pressing concerns or problems regarding your business: cash flow management, taxes, competition, trained employees, general business information, etc.
8. Please rank these benefits of the chamber website: helpfulness, event registration, government relations legislative tracker, RSS feeds, etc.
9. Please rank how the chamber staff is currently doing in the following areas: customer service, responsiveness, communication, billing, explanation of member benefits and support.
10. Please feel free to add any additional comments on how the chamber could improve member experience.

Source: Alexandria Chamber of Commerce, Alexandria, VA.

Membership Management Essentials for Chambers of Commerce.
Edited by Scott C. Stevenson.
© 2012 Stevenson, Inc. Published 2012 by Stevenson, Inc.

Membership Management Essentials for Chambers of Commerce

MEMBER APPRECIATION AND RECOGNITION

The ways in which you show appreciation and dole out well-deserved recognition will impact member retention and serve to raise public awareness of your Chamber and its many benefits. Here are several examples of ways in which chambers all across the country are showcasing and recognizing their members.

Want to Thank and Recognize Members? Take Out an Ad!

Thanking members for their patronage can be a simple process — as simple as taking out an ad in your local newspaper, says Katie DiMaria, executive director, Niles Chamber of Commerce (Niles, IL).

In conjunction with Chamber of Commerce week occurring the second week of September, the Niles Chamber of Commerce takes out a two-page, center-spread ad in the local saturation newspaper, which goes to every home and business in Niles, DiMaria says. The ad lists all 475 chamber members by anniversary date, with some members going back as far as 35 years with the chamber. The banner to the ad thanks the members for their support of the chamber and encourages readers to shop locally.

So what is accomplished with such an ad? The executive director says the ad offers local business owners recognition and visibility for their business while allowing the chamber to show support of its members.

Plus, shoppers are encouraged to keep their business in town.

"The ad is very well received," says DiMaria, noting that any time they can provide an additional service such as this to members that they don't pay extra for is a benefit. "It also helps us to show our appreciation and helps promote their business."

As an added touch, DiMaria arranges to have chamber ambassadors and board members hand-deliver the special issue of the paper to members.

Source: Katie DiMaria, Executive Director, Niles Chamber of Commerce, Niles, IL. E-mail: Katie@nileschamber.com

Include Member Interviews in Newsletter, Magazine

Looking for a fun way to get to know your members? Include lighthearted personal interviews with them in your membership newsletter or magazine.

Officials with the Sanibel & Captiva Islands Chamber of Commerce (Sanibel Island, FL) began including member interviews in its news magazine in 2007.

They print and distribute some 2,000 copies of the magazine every two months.

"This feature came about through one of many creative brainstorming sessions between my husband and me," says Bridgit Stone-Budd, director of marketing.

"I wanted something light and fun, but also informative for our members," Stone-Budd says. "Through research and experience, I've realized that retaining readership is fueled by two things: local interest stories and member photos. Fellow members and business owners enjoy reading about each other."

Interview subjects answer 10 questions created by Stone-Budd. She draws from a pool of questions she crafted, but, she notes, "I do use some particular ones over and over again because I get hilarious answers."

Some of her favorite questions include:

• What did you want to be when you grew up?
• Boxers or briefs?
• Do you like Spam?

To determine which member to interview, she says, "I pick different groups of members, sometimes accommodations, sometimes the board of directors, retail, restaurants, services, etc. Then I e-mail the interview questions to about 10 to 15 in the group in hopes that I can pick at least five good/juicy ones per issue."

When creating interview questions, use a mix of serious and silly questions to create a more dynamic interview.

Source: Bridgit Stone-Budd, Director of Marketing, Sanibel & Captiva Islands Chamber of Commerce, Sanibel Island, FL.

Content not available in this edition

Visits Offer Opportunity to Connect With Members

Visiting your members where they work or live can provide the perfect opportunity to nurture connections and share information — especially when these members have been unable to attend organization meetings or events.

"Each month we visit 10 members whom we haven't seen at an event," says Kori Brady, executive director, Streetsboro Chamber of Commerce (Streetsboro, OH), noting she borrowed the idea from a neighboring chamber.

"The goal of the visits is to let members know they're important to us and see if there is anything we can do for them," Brady says. "We ask if there are particular reasons why they can't make meetings. We inform them of discounts and anything else they might not be aware of."

A chamber official gives the member half of a playing card and invites him/her to an upcoming chamber luncheon, telling the member that the other half will go in a drawing with those of other members. The member whose card is drawn gets a free lunch (value: $15).

The visits are proven retention tools, says Brady, noting that a database helps track member visits.

Visits are conducted by Brady and a member of the chamber's volunteer membership committee. She notes that the committee members find the visits beneficial, "because they also hand out their business cards and other members recognize them when they come to the next event. They also have the opportunity to promote their own business."

The visits strengthen member-organization ties, she says: "We encourage them to become involved and active members. They might not be able to make the meetings because of their schedules, but they know we haven't forgotten about marketing them."

Source: Kori Brady, Executive Director, Streetsboro Chamber of Commerce, Streetsboro, OH.

Welcome New Members With Visits to Their Businesses

Visiting new members is a great way to welcome them into your organization and introduce them to your staff.

"I make it a goal to visit every new member," says Dr. Ruth Couch, executive director, Beebe Chamber of Commerce (Beebe, AR). "The ostensible purpose is to take them their membership plaque, but I also share information about our activities and try to answer any questions they may have."

Couch says she tries to visit members soon after they join but doesn't have a set schedule.

"I take a plaque to all who are located in Beebe," she says. Out-of-town members (25 percent of chamber membership) receive plaques by mail.

"The visits strengthen the relationships, because I tell members to get in touch with me if they have a concern or want to share anything," says Couch. "They have a face to put with the voice, and so do I. I can give them a special invitation to our meetings and other events. In addition, becoming acquainted with them and their services helps me when newcomers inquire about services. I may be able to refer a newcomer to a new member."

Source: Dr. Ruth Couch, Executive Director, Beebe Chamber of Commerce, Beebe, AR.
E-mail: chamber@beebeark.org

Thank Members With VIP Programs

Looking for a way to thank certain members for their participation and support? Consider creating a VIP program that provides a select group of members with additional benefits and services.

In February 2008, staff with the Lake Champlain Regional Chamber of Commerce (Burlington, VT) created a VIP program for members who frequently attended their business after-hours networking events.

"We wanted to do something that thanked our regular business after hours attendees and highlighted them to the other members," says Susan B. Fayette, director of member development and benefits.

The VIP program application asks for a $45 one-time fee, basic contact information, credit card information to process the $45 fee to cover program costs and also if the applicant would like a coupon book at a discounted price.

VIP program recipients receive:

✓ A permanent nametag with chamber lanyard to wear at all events.
✓ A $10 discount on the chamber's $60 coupon books.

✓ Walk-in price of $8 per event ticket, a $4 savings per ticket.
✓ Entry in a monthly drawing featuring sponsor-donated prizes such as restaurant gift certificates.
✓ An invitation to the chamber's annual VIP-only luncheon, which is paid for by a sponsor and is free to attend.
✓ Placement of the VIP member's name and company on the VIP page of the chamber's website.
✓ Special check-in at events, which includes the member's nametag waiting for them at the check-in table, regardless of whether they have pre-registered.

As of May 2009, some 20 members had signed on for the VIP program. Fayette says members often ask how they can become part of the VIP program when they see their fellow members receiving the VIP treatment at events. For the most part, the program has become invitation only, with Fayette reaching out to members at the business after hours events to let them know how they can join the program.

Source: Susan B. Fayette, Director of Member Development and Benefits, Lake Champlain Regional Chamber of Commerce, Burlington, VT. E-mail: susanb@vermont.org

Membership Management Essentials for Chambers of Commerce

Spotlight Tables Showcase Members

At the Pewaukee Chamber of Commerce (Pewaukee, WI) new members get the opportunity to host a Spotlight Table at monthly membership meetings where existing and new members can learn more about their business. One business member is selected as the chamber's Member in Spotlight and offered the opportunity to host the spotlight table and receive a printed bio in the newsletter and a free lunch.

The concept behind the spotlight table is that new featured members host a table at the monthly membership luncheon. The table is filled with brochures, business cards, giveaways and information about the new member's business. As existing members enter the event, they introduce themselves to the new member at the spotlight table and the new member then tells those stopping by about the business they're in, potentially interacting with new customers.

"Spotlight tables give new members a chance to introduce themselves, what they do or sell to the membership and gives the older members a chance to learn what the new member does, and to exchange business cards, in an effort to grow their businesses," says Kathy Eckhardt, executive director of the chamber.

The monthly member-meeting luncheons pull in an average of 65 to 75 of the chamber's 200 members and the numbers continue to increase due to features such as spotlight tables.

Gift Bags Promote, Entice

The Pewaukee Chamber of Commerce (Pewaukee, WI) has introduced new efforts to give new members notice and reward those new members for joining. Beyond adding Spotlight Tables at member events as described at left, new members also receive gift bags upon joining the chamber.

Staff fill the gift bags with promotional items from existing members, which makes this a cost-effective giveaway for the chamber.

"New members love receiving the bags because often the items are practical in nature such as pens or note pads, and it quickly gives them an idea of some of the business owners who are members within the chamber they can do business with," says Eckhardt. "Both the spotlight tables and the gift bags for new members are a way to promote supporting each other within the community."

"New members love this and older members like seeing the new growth in the chamber," says Eckhardt. "We also open these luncheons to the business community and often get one or two new businesses attending who become new members."

Source: Kathy Eckhardt, Executive Director, Pewaukee Chamber of Commerce, Pewaukee, WI. E-mail: info@pewaukeechamber.org.

Prominently Feature Nonprofit Members Serving Constituents

Do all you can to showcase your members — especially those who play an active role in your organization and/or your community.

A visit to the website for the Wayne County Area Chamber of Commerce (Richmond, IN) shows influential nonprofit members listed across the top of the chamber's Web page.

A recent header on the main Web page at www.wcareachamber.org reads: "Non-Profit Partners: Main Street Richmond, Economic Development Corporation, WayNet and Richmond/Wayne County Tourism."

Why would the chamber feel compelled to list these nonprofit member agencies and what purpose does doing so serve?

"We have 60 to 70 nonprofit members," says Suzanne Derengowski, interim CEO. "Those listed at the top of our webpage are countywide nonprofits that serve the county in a development-type role. Like many chambers, we're often a gateway to the community, and we feel it's important to list these agencies that have missions related to ours."

These countywide agencies offer pieces of the puzzle to serving the county and chamber members, says Derengowski. For example, the chamber member WayNet offers a community calendar at its Web page that serves members and potential members of the chamber.

"For those looking to see the complete picture of our community, they would also want to go to the websites of the nonprofits listed," she says.

In addition to featuring these nonprofit agencies on the main page of the website, the chamber links to the agency's website and those agencies link to the chamber's website creating a cohesive look into the community agencies and what they offer members.

Derengowski says featuring member nonprofit organizations in this manner also benefits members through:

- Ability to connect from one website to key community development organizations.
- Better understanding of the connections between key organizations within your community.
- Connections to organizations with coordinating and cohesive missions.

Source: Suzanne Derengowski, Interim CEO, Wayne County Area Chamber of Commerce, Richmond, IN. E-mail: suzanne@wcareachamber.org

Spotlight Members With Access Cable Interview

The New London Area Chamber of Commerce (New London, WI) offers "Meet Our Chamber Members" cable interviews as a unique benefit to interested members.

The interviews are recorded on a monthly basis as time allows. The chamber's monthly newsletter notifies members of taping dates that are available and the members contact the chamber staff to book their interviews.

Since initiating this benefit in April 2010, the chamber has conducted 30 member interviews which are aired on the city's local cable channel.

The chamber's Executive Director, Laurie Shaw, conducts all of the interviews, as she embodies what the chamber is all about, says Corinne Sommer, information specialist for the chamber. "For viewers, it provides a sense of familiarity, as well."

Each interview — approximately 15 minutes in length — is recorded by a city cable access employee. The interviews are then aired initially for a two-week time period and after that they are used as fillers between cable programming throughout the year.

"The spots can be viewed from our city's website and the city is currently in the process of uploading them on Blip TV which will then allow us to link to them from our chamber member's listing on the chamber's website," says Sommer.

Sommer shares a few tips for making the most of cable interviews as a member benefit:

- "While we do provide a list of standard questions, we encourage our members to provide their own questions that will bring out information they want to share during the interview."
- Have the same person conduct the interviews to promote consistency and a fluid transition from one interview to the next.
- Work cohesively with your city staff to form a partnership that allows for free interviewing of members and airing of their segments.

Source: Corinne Sommer, Information Specialist II, New London Area Chamber of Commerce, New London, WI.
E-mail: Corinne@newlondonwi.org

Chamber TV Offers One-stop Viewing

Looking for a new member benefit? Let members be a TV star.

The Salem Area Chamber of Commerce (Salem, OR) has a portion of its website where members can post business-related video for all to see.

This portion of the website is titled ChamberTV, and members can post YouTube videos of activities or events that have taken place in their businesses. This dedicated page allows members to post news clips, event video, videos of volunteers in action, training videos or any other relevant clips. Additionally, chamber training videos and tutorials can be found on this page, offering one-stop convenient viewing for browsers of the site.

According to Kyle Sexton, director of business development for the chamber, this type of sticky content causes a visitor to pause and take extra time when stopping by your site.

Built on Ning technology (www.ning.com), the page allows members to post videos directly to the Web page. The videos are then automatically loaded to the chamber's Facebook page and Twitter account.

Videos posted on ChamberTV can contain a full text description, and even links, to improve the search engine optimization of the video's content.

Sexton offers the following tips for offering a Web page like ChamberTV:

- Create a video tutorial to demonstrate how simple it is to post a video from YouTube to your site.
- Ask your video production company members to post their work and any videos they produce, to give your members an example of what is possible. This also gives the production companies a chance to promote their work.
- Teach your members best practices in video production in case they would like to produce their own videos. Most computers come with free video production software that is simple to use. Additionally, many high definition video cameras are low-cost.

Source: Kyle Sexton, Director of Business Development, Salem Area Chamber of Commerce, Salem, OR.
E-mail: kyle@salemchamber.org

Offer Specialty Awards to Exceptional Members

Always be on the lookout for ways to recognize and share member accomplishments.

Staff with the Fox Cities Chamber of Commerce (Appleton, WI) grant specialty awards to members who contribute to the community, says Pamela Hull, vice president-membership & operations.

One such honor is the Athena Award, given annually to an exceptional businesswoman who: 1) has achieved the highest degree of professional excellence; 2) has assisted women in reaching their potential; and 3) possesses an impactful body of work.

"The Athena Award honors women business leaders for their exceptional contributions to their company, their industry, their community, to their chamber and to the advancement of women in business," Hull says. She adds that the chamber is among the charter group of chambers to host the awards since the program's inception in 1985.

More information about the Athena Award is available at www.athenafoundation.org.

Source: Pamela Hull, Vice President-Membership & Operations Manager, Fox Cities Chamber of Commerce, Appleton, WI. E-mail: phull@foxcitieschamber.com

Honor Member Anniversaries In Numerous Ways

Recognizing members' ongoing commitment and loyalty to your organization is a simple but key component in membership retention.

Officials with the Sioux Falls Area Chamber of Commerce (Sioux Falls, SD) recognize member anniversaries by posting them prominently on the main page of the organization's website (www.siouxfallschamber.com). Selecting the "Click Here For Member Anniversaries" button tab takes website visitors to a listing of member milestone anniversaries taking place that month.

Betty Ordal, membership services director, offers the following tips for honoring member anniversaries, based on ways the chamber celebrates these important members:

✓ **Send a personalized letter to arrive near the anniversary date.** The chamber sends a letter signed by the chamber president pointing out the chamber's and the member's accomplishments.

✓ **Offer members a memento to recognize their anniversaries.** At the chamber, members may request a plaque signifying the years they have been members. The plaque depicts a background of the waterfall the area is known for and is mounted on a cherrywood frame. Ordal says that many members display all anniversary plaques in their businesses or can replace a five-year plaque with a 10-year plaque, for example.

✓ **Personalize gift delivery.** At the chamber, staff hand-deliver anniversary plaques during unannounced visits. Ordal says the surprise acknowledgement is a welcome treat to members and allows chamber staff to become better acquainted with members and member businesses.

✓ **Recognize anniversaries in publications.** Member anniversaries are noted in the chamber newsletter, which is inserted into the local newspaper (30,000 circulation) the first Monday of each month and mailed to 5,000 chamber members.

✓ **Use annual dues payment to recognize anniversaries.** Member anniversaries take place one year from the date of inception at the Sioux Falls Area Chamber, therefore, when annual membership dues are paid, this signifies member anniversary dates as well. When dues are paid, the chamber membership staff sends an e-mail thanking members for continuing their membership. Ordal says staff members often reply to this e-mail with specific information on the trends of their business.

> The Web page that celebrates member anniversaries at the Sioux Falls Area Chamber of Commerce (Sioux Falls, SD) includes the lead-in paragraph, below. Member listings feature links to information on each business and its website:
>
> ### April Member Anniversaries
>
> Congratulations to the following members who are celebrating their 25-plus, 20-, 15-, 10- and five-year membership anniversaries this month. They are part of a continued commitment to our community through their investment in the Sioux Falls Area Chamber of Commerce. To learn more about Chamber membership, contact 605.336.1620 or sfacc@siouxfalls.com.

Source: Betty Ordal, Membership Services Director, Sioux Falls Area Chamber of Commerce, Sioux Falls, SD. E-mail: bordal@siouxfalls.com

Membership Management Essentials for Chambers of Commerce.
Edited by Scott C. Stevenson.
© 2012 Stevenson, Inc. Published 2012 by Stevenson, Inc.

Membership Management Essentials for Chambers of Commerce

What sorts of fundraising events and projects has your chamber taken on in the past? Are their any that are particularly unique to your organization? Check out these eight examples of chamber events and projects that have worked for these organizations.

Gaming Tips Make Casino Night a Winner

The Oregon Area Chamber of Commerce (Oregon, WI) hosts an annual award banquet to honor its shining star members. In addition to presenting awards to deserving chamber members, the evening boasts a casino gaming portion that provides lively entertainment for guests.

Kristin McGuine, member services manager and event planner for the annual awards dinner, shares tips for introducing casino gaming to an event:

- ✓ Locate and interview gaming outfitters in your area. The Oregon Area Chamber of Commerce works with a company named Vegas Nights (Spring Green, WI) that provides professional tables, props and dealers. Be sure to request black jack tables, craps tables, roulette or other specific casino games.
- ✓ Enlist services of an outfitter who will offer educational opportunities for guests during the gaming portion of the night. At the annual awards dinner, a craps table is available for play and allows guests to learn a new game with help from the professional dealers.
- ✓ Choose a venue that will allow ample room for gaming. Planners provide seating at the gaming tables for 85 percent of the night's total guests. For the 130 guests who attend this awards dinner and gaming night, 110 seats are available at gaming tables for those participating in the casino portion of the evening.
- ✓ Determine how prizes will be distributed. During the casino portion of the evening, guests win chips that are converted to raffle tickets. Guests can then drop their raffle tickets into a goblet near an auction item for a chance to win the item during a drawing. The more tickets a guest wins, the more chances they have to win that item.

Source: Kristin McGuine, Member Services Manager, Oregon Area Chamber of Commerce, Oregon, WI. E-mail: staff@oregonwi.com

Offer Additional Fun For Non-gaming Guests

The Annual Awards Dinner presented by the Oregon Area Chamber of Commerce (Oregon, WI) offers casino gaming as the entertainment portion of their evening. But what about guests who aren't gamers?

Recognizing that not all guests will be interested in gaming or some will want to take breaks from the fun, chamber officials also offer a dessert reception during the gaming portion of the evening. A dessert reception area is created offering guests sweet treats such as pie, cake and chocolates from a local professional chocolatier.

The dessert reception is located in a nearby but separate area away from the gaming section to give guests a quiet area to visit and relax, says Kristin McGuine, member services manager.

Offer a Buy a Brick Competition

Staff with the Atmore Area Chamber of Commerce (Atmore, AL) offer a simple way to honor area citizens and historical events while raising funds: selling bricks through the aptly named campaign, Buy a Brick!

Gregg Akins, board member, came up with the idea to allow area residents to go to the chamber website to purchase memorial bricks for $100 each. The 4 X 8-inch bricks can be laser-engraved with up to three lines of text the donor chooses. Chamber staff work with Bricks 'R Us (Miami, FL) to create the bricks. The company also lists a link to Atmore's campaign at its website for customer ease. To reduce shipping costs, the chamber waits until 25 bricks are sold before ordering a shipment.

To add healthy competition to the campaign, board members split into three groups with the goal of selling $3,000 worth or 30 of the memorial bricks per team.

As bricks are sold and engraved, Atmore residents replace the paver bricks outside of Atmore's historic post office with the engraved memorial bricks.

Akins says he hopes to make this an ongoing effort for the chamber, and recommends other member organizations try the concept, which he describes as "effortless."

Source: Gregg Akins, Board Member, Atmore Area Chamber of Commerce, Atmore, AL. E-mail: atmoreal@frontier.net

Get Corporate Teams to Participate in Your Run

If you're planning a run/walk event, why not get local businesses to encourage their employees to lace up their shoes.

The Tour of the Gables 5K (Coral Gables, FL) had more than 20 local businesses participate in the 2011 race, more than half of which had at least five runners/walkers on their team. "In our case, as a chamber of commerce, it fits our mission of corporate engagement while building community," says Mark Trowbridge, president and CEO of the Coral Gables Chamber of Commerce.

So what is the best way to recruit corporate teams? Trowbridge advises planning early and reaching out to businesses even earlier. "We begin about 10 months out with a focus group of previous runners, get their feedback, and begin to work with local companies on sponsorship and supporting teams," he says.

When approaching a company, Trowbridge suggests working through the HR department. When talking to the HR personnel, he says to focus on the run/walk as both a team building exercise and a wellness activity for employees. "I think all companies are great candidates, but certainly those that already have wellness programs or incentives and do community events are great partners," he says.

The Tour of the Gables 5K also provides an added incentive — the corporate team with the most runners wins the Chairman's Cup.

"They receive a trophy and their team photo goes in our promotional brochure the next year," says Trowbridge.

Source: Mark Trowbridge, President and CEO, Coral Gables Chamber of Commerce, Coral Gables, FL. E-mail: info@coralgableschamber.org

Content not available in this edition

Use a flyer like this one to build corporate support for your run/walk event.

Member-driven Fundraiser Raises Eyebrows, Funds

What do you call an auto dealer standing naked except for one strategically placed hubcap?

Or how about a real estate agent enjoying a cigar and glass of wine with nothing more than a For Sale sign for cover?

The Greater Westerly-Pawcatuck Chamber of Commerce (Westerly, RI) calls it fundraising.

"They're all chamber members and basically naked except for a prop representing their business to cover their 'business,'" says Lisa Konicki, chamber executive director, of the chamber's popular Men of Westerly calendar fundraiser. "They get some great publicity; they help the chamber,;and they raise money for some good causes, too."

The fundraiser, now in its second year, is planned and produced by the chamber, but proceeds are shared with several local charities, adding to the fundraiser's appeal and area impact.

The 2010 calendar featured 33 local businessmen ranging in age from late 20s to early 70s.

"It's not about physical appearance," says Konicki, re-

calling the standing ovation received by the calendar's two over-70 models. "Featuring people with a solid reputation in the community, guys everybody knows and loves, is what really makes it work."

Because models are sworn to secrecy and photographed outside normal business hours, speculation fuels much of the buzz surrounding the event. A gala event — Men of Westerly Revealed — taps this curiosity with a grand reveal of the participating businessmen and an unveiling of the new calendar.

"Done right, it's something the community can really get behind," Konicki says. "It's fun, humorous and all about having a big heart."

Not only did the calendar project celebrate and spotlight members and the chamber throughout the community and beyond, Konicki says, it helped raise significant funds. The 2009 calendar sales, combined with ticket sales, sponsorship and advertising, netted around $13,000.

Source: Lisa Konicki, Executive Director, The Greater Westerly-Pawcatuck Chamber of Commerce, Westerly, RI.
E-mail: Lkonicki@westerlychamber.org

Vendor Application Process Secures Cream of the Crop

To find high-quality, professional food vendors for the Brighton Smokin' Jazz & Barbecue Blues Festival (Brighton, MI), the Greater Brighton Area Chamber of Commerce (Brighton, MI) goes through a stringent review of all applicants.

Each year, chamber officials sift through hundreds of applications to hone in on the top 20 vendors who will participate in the festival. This annual event — last slated for Sept. 9-10, 2011 — regularly draws nearly 30,000 guests.

Food vendors complete an application (shown at right) and prepare a presentation packet, complete with photos, for the committee and members of the chamber to peruse.

Chamber Director of Events, Rebecca Boss shares tips for selecting food vendors for your next festival or other special event:

✓ When sending out applications, include an informational page about requirements and restrictions. Be specific about your event up front. You don't want any surprises!

✓ Require food vendors to complete a detailed application that includes booth rental selection, menu, photo request and food permit requirements, if applicable.

✓ Ask applicants to send an application fee to cover expenses incurred by the application review. The Brighton Chamber requires fees of $10 to $20 to cover these expenses.

✓ Have vendors prepare a presentation packet that includes photos of their booth setup and details about foods they will prepare at your event. Also, require that they send a menu and list of ingredients that will be prepared at the event.

✓ Prep your review committee to look for quality, professional presentation; lean toward choosing established vendors.

✓ When reviewing applications with your committee, make sure that you are selecting a variety of food options for your attendees.

Content not available in this edition

Source: Rebecca Boss, Director of Events, Greater Brighton Area Chamber of Commerce, Brighton, MI. E-mail: Beccab@brightoncoc.org.

Integrate Marketing Initiatives to Secure Sponsorships

With non-dues revenue fast becoming membership organizations' bread and butter, sponsorship opportunities will only grow in importance, says Ann Ormond, president of the Greater Newburyport Chamber of Commerce & Industry (Newburyport, MA), which has a strategy to integrate hard copy and online presentations of sponsorship opportunities.

Central to the strategy are single-page flyers detailing chamber sponsorship opportunities. Given to potential sponsors, these flyers, such as the two shown at right, highlight event activities, key exposure points and sponsorship ranges. Staff also bind a year's worth of flyers into booklets to share with top supporters.

Electronic advertising augments these efforts. Sponsored events are featured in posts that offer a brief description, expected attendance and price range, and a link to the full sponsorship flyer. Ormond estimates website postings generate three to six sponsorships a month while requiring minimal staff time.

To draw potential sponsors, Ormond recommends stating as much critical information as possible. "Put the price out front," she says, "and if it's in the ball park, people will call."

She also recommends moving completed events to the bottom of the Web page — not deleting them — to build event awareness.

Source: Ann Ormond, President, Greater Newburyport Chamber of Commerce & Industry, Newburyport, MA.
E-mail: aormond@newburyportchamber.org

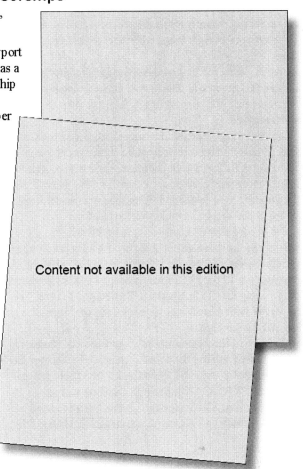
Content not available in this edition

Add a Theme to Boost Your Auction's Success

Staff with the Greater Topsail Area Chamber of Commerce and Tourism (Surf City, NC) have honed hosting auction events. Recently, they presented a 17th annual auction that brought in 175 guests and $10,000 while promoting area and local businesses.

This year's Beach Party theme gave an element of light-hearted excitement for attendees who bid on beach bags, sailboat décor, nautical lamps, a boat cruise, golf membership and more.

Here are some new ideas to try for your next auction event:

- Call on business members for donations assuming a do-nated item has already been selected. "We call on current business members and ask what they've decided to contribute for the auction instead of asking if they're willing to contribute," says Laura Bageant, event organizer.

- Remind auction contributors that donating to the auction will bring positive exposure to their business through advertising and promotion of the event.

- Play a slide show flashing contributors' logos during the silent auction. Logos should flash on the screen along with information about businesses that contribute to the auction to both promote local business and thank those who donated items. Use the slide show during the live auction as well to bring more tangible value and interest to auction items such as tickets or weekend getaways.

Source: Laura Bageant, Event Organizer, The Greater Topsail Area Chamber of Commerce and Tourism, Surf City, NC.
E-mail: info@topsailcoc.com

Host Ancillary Events That Reinforce Your Mission

Consider making your membership events more meaningful by aligning your event's focus with your organization's mission.

For six years, the Colorado Women's Chamber of Commerce (Denver, CO) has hosted a female-supportive leadership event that supports and reinforces its own female-forward mission.

Orchestrating Leadership works to advance the career path of female musical conductors through a mentorship opportunity with Conductor Laureate Marin Alsop, founder of Taki Concordia Conducting Fellowship. The overall vision of the program is to foster and encourage women who are studying or training to be orchestral conductors.

The event features a truly unique benefit where members can purchase an event ticket at a discounted rate to experience a day of orchestral charm, including a behind-the-scenes glimpse of the Colorado Symphony while witnessing Alsop tutoring the Taki Concordia Conducting Fellow. The event wraps with a luncheon, where guests can interact with Alsop and her protégé.

"This event has a great tie-in to our mission of creating an environment and the resources conducive to our member's business success," says Elizabeth Leake, event and project manager for CWCC. "With a strong focus on women mentoring women, Orchestrating Leadership allows our members to watch as a seasoned, successful woman guides and mentors a young woman who is growing her skills and career. It also provides the opportunity for some of our members to get personally involved by providing specialized workshops for the mentee throughout the week."

To make this event happen successfully year after year, the chamber calls on its most trusted and significant sponsors to help with the expenses of bringing the young conductor to Denver to share in this once-in-a-lifetime opportunity for aspiring conductors. The chamber also forged a significant bond with Alsop who was the first female conductor to head a major American symphony and who is an active member of the chamber, to create this unique and inspiring annual event.

To ensure that your events align with your organization's mission, ask yourself these questions in the planning phase:

- In what three ways can we introduce aspects to the event that will forward our mission?

- Which guest speaker or featured guest would best convey our organization's message?

- What target audience from our membership will benefit most from this event, and what is the best channel to reach this target group when promoting the event?

Source: Elizabeth Leake, Event and Project Manager, Colorado Women's Chamber of Commerce, Denver, CO. E-mail: eleake@cwcc.org

Online Seating Chart Helps Sell Tickets to Member Events

Here's a member-pleasing way to increase ticket sales for your next sit-down event: Put a seating chart on your website and let members choose where they will sit.

That's what officials with the Traverse City Area Chamber of Commerce (Traverse City, MI) did for the first time last year, and according to Communications Coordinator Nate Jorgensen, every limited-seating event that used the chart in 2010 was sold out.

Jorgensen uses the software program Adobe Photoshop to create the chart (shown at right), creating different layers to represent the available and reserved seats. The website is updated daily to show who is sitting at what table.

"The chart shows how the event is filling up and encourages members and guests to buy their tickets," says Jorgensen.

Chamber staff use the same techniques to create a virtual version of its annual business expo.

Source: Nate Jorgensen, Communications Coordinator, Traverse City Area Chamber of Commerce, Traverse City, MI. E-mail: jorgensen@tcchamber.org

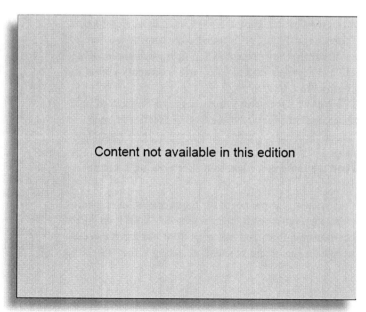

Content not available in this edition

Membership Management Essentials for Chambers of Commerce

EVALUATING PROGRAMS AND IMPROVING MEMBER RELATIONS

Evaluation should be an ongoing process for any Chamber of Commerce — evaluation of recruitment and retention procedures, evaluation of member programs and services, evaluation of the ways in which you communicate with members and more. And a key aspect of evaluation should include seeking member feedback. Give your members a strong voice in the direction your chamber takes as it moves forward.

Seek Member Input to Help Shape Benefit Offerings

Involving members in development and review of new benefits will allow them to take a more vested interest in your organization and ensure that the benefits are worthwhile.

Staff at the Greater Miami Chamber of Commerce (Miami, FL) created a member benefits board committee several years ago that is responsible for identifying new benefits and opportunities for members, says Barry Johnson, president/CEO.

The six-member committee meets monthly to review and recommend benefits to the executive committee that both fill member needs and provide a financial contribution to the chamber. Generally, this committee is provided with offers from member companies by the vice president of marketing and membership services.

The committee decides which offerings would be beneficial to include as member benefits and creates a proposal for the executive committee, which ultimately makes the final decision. The proposal, Johnson notes must "demonstrate the advantages, liabilities and overall benefits of the program."

Recent benefits added through this process include pre-paid legal services, shipping discounts, discounted executive physicals and a new e-based program to help small businesses meet federal requirements for employee training.

A member survey is one tool the committee uses to determine which benefits would be most rewarding.

In April 2007, the committee sent an electronic survey to members, using zoomerang.com, to identify benefits members deemed as most desired and useful. The survey contained eight questions, asking members which benefits and services they were currently aware of and using, and which ones they would like to see in the future. The chamber received 18 responses.

Including members in the benefit development process through surveys and other means makes sense, Johnson says. "The process ensures that the organization is truly reflective of member interest, not just management directive."

For member organizations looking for ways to include members in the benefit review process, Johnson offers this advice: "Members need to be educated on the organization's process for adding new programs so there is an understanding of ground rules and expectations. It would be a major mistake to just involve members to help and not give them the information necessary for them to be able to actually see their contribution make a difference.

"In other words, if the engagement is just superficial and the recommendations made to the organization are not taken seriously, that could damage relationships between the member and the organization. In addition, the organization must ensure that they have put in place the correct steps so that members are not adding programs that may not offer true benefits."

Source: Barry E. Johnson, President/CEO, Greater Miami Chamber of Commerce, Miami, FL. E-mail: bjohnson@miamichamber.com

Online Survey Questionnaires — Getting Member Feedback

The Fox Cities Chamber of Commerce (Appleton, WI) has introduced an opportunity to its members in order to receive feedback. In December, the chamber initiated an online survey that can be completed with anonymity by members to provide unabashed feedback to the chamber.

The member satisfaction survey is designed to take up little time for the survey taker while providing the chamber a wealth of information on how it is doing in the eyes of its members.

"The member satisfaction survey asks all members to rate such things as benefits offered through the chamber, programs to grow the economy, community development involvement, membership events and communications material," says Pamela Hull, vice president-membership & operations. "It is important to take measure in what our membership is all about."

The online survey asks 10 pointed questions, including:

1. How would you assess the value you derive from chamber membership?
2. Which chamber affinity programs do you use?
3. How would you rate the value of the benefits listed above?
4. How would you rate membership events?
5. How would you rate the events and/or programs for economic development and legislative action?
6. How would you rate chamber communications?
7. How would you rate the responsiveness and professionalism of the chamber staff?
8. How would you assess the overall effectiveness of the chamber as an organization?
9. What input can you provide regarding priorities the chamber should address?
10. Is there anything the chamber can do to better serve your firm?

Response options range from excellent to poor and some questions include the rating of a variety of subcategories such as listing specific events offered by the chamber that can be rated under question No. 4.

Chamber staff calls on members during their Project Thank You campaign and ask that members complete the survey. To date, 6 percent of the chamber's 1,700 members have completed the survey. In an effort to bring up that response rate, Hull and her staff will call on members one more time to ask that they respond to the survey.

After compiling the survey results, Hull will then discuss the results with the board and staff to set forth with any adjustments needed to better the chamber.

Source: Pamela Hull, Vice President-Membership & Operations, Fox Cities Chamber of Commerce, Appleton, WI. E-mail: phull@foxcitieschamber.com

Resolving Member Conflicts

When a major dispute arises between your members, it may be beneficial to get involved and offer resolutions.

That's what Tracey M. Lukasik, executive director, Kenmore-Town of Tonawanda Chamber of Commerce (Kenmore, NY), did when she learned of a conflict between two chamber members who rented space in the same plaza.

"There was an issue over parking for their respective customers," Lukasik explains. "An altercation ensued and one of the members came to me to report it. I advised her to file a police report so that a record of events was established in case the situation escalated."

After the situation was brought to the chamber's attention, Lukasik wrote an article in the chamber newsletter referring to it. Rather than list member names, she called them parties "A" and "B."

"I offered some suggestions and tried to make party B see that his actions were unprofessional," she says. "Party B was not happy that I did not call to get his side of the story, so I wrote him a letter of apology but also asked that if the event in question did not really occur, then I would need to know

this. I did not hear back from him."

While Lukasik did not receive additional feedback from either party, she did hear from several members "who were happy that the problem was brought to light. They too were experiencing the same issues with shared public parking lots and thought it was a bigger problem than people realized."

One member involved in the incident chose not to renew their membership; however Lukasik did not know if this was due to this conflict or other reasons.

If faced with a similar situation, Lukasik says she would interview or speak with both parties before commenting on it, as hearing both sides of the story is important to assess the severity of the situation, "I would suggest that both parties talk with an unbiased third person present and try to reach a compromise or agreement, and when applicable, involve the landlord or even law enforcement as a final resort if no resolution can be made."

Source: Tracey M. Lukasik, Executive Director, Kenmore-Town of Tonawanda Chamber of Commerce, Kenmore, NY. E-mail: info@ken-ton.org

Deal With Dissatisfaction by Listening, Creating Resolutions

When faced with dissatisfied members, react by listening and providing positive solutions. Resist the urge to counter members' negative feedback until you have digested their concerns.

"One of the best ways to ensure the majority of our members are happy is to simply listen to what they have to say," says Shawna Grieger, membership director, Grand Junction Area Chamber of Commerce (Grand Junction, CO). "It is true that word of mouth spreads faster than fire, so when a member is disgruntled about his or her membership, we usually catch it pretty fast and follow up with the member to help find a solution. It is very important to ask that member for a solution recommendation so we can keep on the listening side instead of the justification side."

The chamber has six staff members to deal with the needs of 1,300 members.

"We often forget that listening is not talking but letting the other person talk, and hearing what they have to say. If a member came to us and said, 'I invested in this organization and I did not see any benefits,' it would be easy to tell that member what they did wrong or did not take advantage of. A better method is to ask what the member felt was the reason and offer solutions or information to help correct the problem, such as programs the member did not know about or marketing materials that the member could benefit from that was different than what they were using before."

Even after a conflict has been resolved, it is important to maintain a dialogue with members to ensure the solutions you have provided are working. "We always let the members know what our next steps will be and check to make sure there are no lingering concerns after a solution is recommended. If we recommend programs to members as a solution, we usually schedule a reminder to be sent to them before the suggested event so they have an opportunity to participate."

Grieger recommends two methods the chamber uses to remain aware of situations that may cause members to become displeased, saying:

- Give members all-electronic publications and let them decide to opt out if they do not wish to receive the information. This way, it is their decision not to receive the information and no one feels left out.

- Use your staff or volunteers to do annual phone calls or checks on each member before his/her anniversary date. This gives individual attention at least once a year and you can combat any retention problems early; don't ignore a problem.

Finally, remember that when it comes to members, there are no small concerns. Treat every issue with the same amount of immediacy, Grieger says.

"What seems small and trivial to you might be huge to the member, so always immediately follow up with an acknowledgement or possible solution," she says. "The best way of keeping the majority of members happy is to listen to them. You will not be able to please everyone, but you can include the members in resolutions and implementations, and please most."

Source: Shawna Grieger, Membership Director, Grand Junction Area Chamber of Commerce, Grand Junction, CO.

Networking Opportunities Keep Members Coming Back

Want to know what current or potential benefits your members most appreciate?

Ask them.

Through a member survey, staff of the Greater Fort Wayne Chamber of Commerce (Fort Wayne, IN) learned that most members join the chamber for the frequent networking opportunities it offers — networking opportunities that, in many cases, lead to jobs.

Nicole Wilkins, communications manager, says 90 percent of the chamber's 2,000 members are small business owners to whom networking is a key component to their livelihood. "Networking has become a staple to the business of a chamber," Wilkins says. "The chamber remains the place for members to network and build their business."

She cites two specific ways the chamber offers members the opportunity to hone their networking skills:

- High Speed Networking events in which members deliver their "elevator speech" to 21 other members within the course of an hour;

- A Meet Me at 5 event that draws anywhere from 100 to 400 members to mingle for a bit of business while enjoying a unique venue.

To maximize the success of the events, Wilkins says, the chamber uses two critical tools to keep things running smoothly:

1. **Constant Contact** (www.constantcontact.com) — This e-mail system allows chamber staff to send e-blasts to all members about upcoming chamber offerings, and also offers e-mail marketing and online survey features that are useful for disseminating and obtaining information from members.

2. **WebLink** (www.weblinkinternational.com) — This database management software allows members to RSVP and pay for events on the chamber's website and offers tools for running reports useful for event management.

Source: Nicole Wilkins, Communications Manager, The Greater Fort Wayne Chamber of Commerce, Fort Wayne, IN. E-mail: nwilkins@fwchamber.org

Rev Your Members' Engines with a Tune-up

Just like a mechanic's tune-up can keep your car purring, a membership program tune-up can help guarantee your members are happy and all systems are running smoothly.

To keep their membership program coasting along, staff with the West Des Moines Chamber of Commerce (West Des Moines, IA) actually perform membership tune-ups.

Every two months, the chamber offers prospective, new and existing members an opportunity to reignite the drive to maximize their membership potential. Tune-up sessions include approximately 100 invited guests who learn all the details of membership through the chamber.

The chamber president and staff dress in white auto mechanic uniforms adorned with their names and call themselves the service team.

The membership tune-up covers these seven topics:

1. **Recharging Batteries** — discusses networking opportunities through the chamber.

2. **Dust off the Manual** — features an ambassador review of the educational programs available at the chamber.

3. **Insure Your Investment** — covers business referrals and services provided to members by the chamber.

4. **Put the Spark in Your Plugs** — educates members to take advantage of promotional/sponsorship opportunities.

5. **Put Rubber to the Road** — covers committees and task forces members can join.

6. **Map Your Journey** — a staff review of the chamber's website and all that it offers members.

Create Your Own Membership Tune-up

Follow these tips for engaging the audience with your own membership tune-up:

- Keep it light and limit it to about one hour.
- Offer different membership faces throughout presentations. Include staff and ambassadors.
- Present a lively Microsoft PowerPoint presentation to keep the audience's attention.
- Use an interactive online system in which membership staff can interact with the chamber's website to keep the audience engaged.

7. **Get Out of Town** — a thorough explanation of the relationship of affiliate chamber partners throughout the city of Des Moines (a larger city adjacent to West Des Moines) and how they can be beneficial to members.

The presentation takes about an hour — perfect timing for a membership tune-up, according to Linda Hulleman, executive director of the chamber. The tune-up is offered at multiple and varied times throughout the same day to accommodate schedules of all members and to reach out to different segments of the membership.

"This has been a great recruiting and retention tool for our chamber," Hulleman says. "It's proven to be a great way to keep our members engaged, informed and in tune with all of the opportunities we offer to assist in promoting their businesses."

Source: Linda Hulleman, Executive Director, West Des Moines Chamber of Commerce, West Des Moines, IA.
E-mail: LHulleman@wdmleaders.org

Organize a Website Committee

At the Woodbury Chamber of Commerce (Woodbury, MN), a website committee ensures the chamber's website is user-friendly and current for its 310 members.

The four to five committee members offer Web update recommendations and perform technical operation updates while learning new skills, expressing ideas and offering connectivity to the community.

To create such a website committee:

- Seek out members within your nonprofit who are in the field of information technology or Web development to lead this committee.
- Establish a clear, concise action plan for the committee.

- Determine the committee's level of access to your site. For example, full access would allow its members to perform backups and updates as needed.
- Assign one or two members of the committee to test updates for accuracy and usability.
- Assign a staffer the responsibility of reviewing the effectiveness of the website committee and ensure that regular updates are occurring.

Source: Travis Martinson, Executive Director, Woodbury Chamber of Commerce, Woodbury, MN.
E-mail: travis@woodburychamber.org

Is It Time to Retire Your Member Event?

How do you know when it is time to cancel a member event? Use your members feedback — or lack thereof — to guide you.

Staff with the Kirkwood-Des Peres Area Chamber of Commerce (St. Louis, MO) recently canceled their bridal showcase after producing the event for six years.

"We hosted a bridal showcase because it was a great revenue producer for the chamber," says Gina March, vice president of marketing. "However, most of the vendors were non-chamber members and we felt that, of all our events, this one least met the mission of our chamber. Not only was it low in member vendor participation, but very few of our 700 members attended."

While the event produced consistent revenue, it never grabbed the interest of a majority of the chamber's members, says March. With member interest and participation lacking, staff began discussing whether to cancel the event in 2006. A major part of the discussion focused on finding an event to not only replace income brought in by the bridal showcase, but prove more appealing to members.

"Events are hard work, and we don't want to be in the special events business just because we've always done it," she says. "We truly want to provide services to our members that will help them grow their businesses."

They discussed the situation with several members from the health field. Based on this feedback — and with board support — they chose to replace the showcase with a health and wellness expo in 2009.

Wondering whether to permanently cancel an event? Take into account the impact doing so will have on your members. Does it fit well with your organization's mission/vision? Would most members miss this event if you were to cancel it? If the answer to these questions is no, it may be time to retire the event. If the answer is yes, reconsider eliminating it.

Source: Gina March, Vice President Marketing, Kirkwood-Des Peres Area Chamber of Commerce, St. Louis, MO.
E-mail: gina@thechamber.us

Emphasize Customer Care With Member Services Committee

Would a member services committee help you provide better service to your members?

At the 1,500-member Pasadena Chamber of Commerce (Pasadena, CA), a member services committee that includes the membership manager and chamber president advises the chamber board on matters related to the support of members, quality and quantity of member opportunities, plus retention and recruitment.

"Part of what the committee does is see how effective the staff is at serving the members' needs, including how we ensure they get their questions answered and how we help them access information and support if we cannot provide it in-house," says Paul Little, president and CEO. "We do as much referring to local agencies and groups that can provide technical support to members as we do providing information directly."

Little shares advice on organizing a member services committee:

❑ Enlist a variety of people who can view the member-serving activities from a wide range of perspectives, including staff and member volunteers.

❑ Make sure members serving on the committee consider the impact new and existing activities have on other businesses as well as their own.

❑ Have committee members consider the role of paid professional staff and how such personnel can best serve the membership.

❑ Encourage committee members to be creative. Encourage free thinking and ideas.

❑ Support the committee's efforts to offer new ideas and try new things to excite, educate and serve the membership.

❑ Offer members an interactive blog or Q&A section on your website to pose questions membership committee members can reply to with tips, advice and resources.

Source: Paul Little, President and CEO, Pasadena Chamber of Commerce, Pasadena, CA.
E-mail: Paul@pasadena-chamber.org

Membership Management Essentials for Chambers of Commerce.
Edited by Scott C. Stevenson.
© 2012 Stevenson, Inc. Published 2012 by Stevenson, Inc.

Membership Management Essentials for Chambers of Commerce

To learn more about what your chamber of commerce can do to grow its membership, achieve more and elevate its reputation, check out what these 11 chambers have done to serve their members and achieve more than they ever thought possible.

Partner With College or University to Begin Member Group

"The most enjoyable project I have worked on in 10 years as a chamber member," is how Jim Giammarinaro, vice chair of membership at MetroWest Chamber of Commerce (Framingham, MA), describes the chamber's recent partnership with Framingham State University.

The chamber wanted to connect with younger members and help young professionals break into the business world. The partnership started with a board member meeting with the president of Framingham State University.

Here is how the program works, according to Giammarinaro and Chamber President and CEO Bonnie Biocchi:

- **The university identifies students who are a good fit for the program.** MetroWest provides marketing collateral to the school to help promote the program. A typical participating student is a junior or senior pursuing a career in business. The plan was to have 10 students. However, the program was so popular that 16 students participated, requiring greater investment from chamber members and the university.

- **Chamber members sponsor students by paying two thirds of the cost of a discounted membership with full benefits.** The sponsorship opportunity appealed to both small businesses and larger corporations. Framingham State University covers the remaining third of the membership cost. The sponsorship lasts for a year, at which point students can become members on their own.

- **Each student is paired with a chamber member who serves as their coach for the year.** Coaches attend chamber meetings to help their student network and meet new contacts. They also meet throughout the year to gauge how the experience is going and provide the students practical career development training. The coaching opportunity has primarily appealed to small and mid-sized companies. Giammarinaro believes coaching could positively impact retention as members become more engaged.

The partnership with Framingham State University was such a success, the chamber has decided to partner with nearby Clark University in the coming year. In this difficult job market, the chamber's partnership with local universities serves as an important bridge between students and future employers. It also provides MetroWest with greater community connections, a more engaged membership, and young, excited members with fresh ideas.

Sources: Jim Giammarinaro, Vice Chair of Membership; Bonnie Biocchi, President and CEO, MetroWest Chamber of Commerce, Framingham, MA. E-mail: jim@freedomdigitalprinting.com; bonnie@metrowest.org

Create a Speakers Bureau to Promote Membership, Members

To promote members and assist the community, staff with the Eastern Montgomery County Chamber of Commerce (EMCCC), Jenkintown, PA, have created a pool of speakers from their membership of 700.

The EMCCC staff created its speakers bureau as a place where members can enroll to become expert speakers for events conducted by the chamber and in the community. Members can apply to become speakers and chamber staff recruit speakers from outside of the organization to continue to build the pool of speakers available and to create opportunities to enlist new members.

"We're always thinking about how we can make connections," says Nancy Ischinger, member services director. "Whenever possible, we draw from our membership for speakers and presenters."

The chamber provides speakers for more than 50 events each year, so the speaker database is useful in providing excellent programs and promoting membership.

Source: Nancy Ischinger, Member Services Director, Eastern Montgomery County Chamber of Commerce, Jenkintown, PA. E-mail: Nancy@emccc.org

Promote Membership Via Speakers Bureau

Consider building a speakers bureau to build and promote your membership. Here's how:

- ✓ Attend a presentation that features a highly recommended speaker. Recruit this person as a potential speakers bureau candidate and future member of your organization.
- ✓ Ask members for seminar referrals. If members have attended seminars that offered excellent presentations by speakers, ask your members to refer those speakers for building your speakers bureau.
- ✓ Offer excellent seminars and programs within your organization and the speakers will follow.
- ✓ Continue to build a database of speakers so you are always ready to answer requests for speakers.
- ✓ Promote your speakers bureau throughout your community to solicit interest and turn those interested presenters into members.

Member Boot Camp Brings Together Women Entrepreneurs

Few perks beat the opportunity to have a great time, meet new friends and gain useful information to help you succeed, personally and professionally.

That's the benefit female members of the Greater Phoenix Chamber of Commerce (Phoenix, AZ) enjoy by taking part in the Women Entrepreneurs Small Business Boot Camp. Chamber officials partner with Susan Ratliff Presents LLC (Phoenix, AZ) to offer members and local female entrepreneurs the daylong boot camp of education and motivation.

The boot camp offers a powerful day of world-class insights, cutting-edge success strategies, practical tools and relevant topics for women in business. Drawing some 200 attendees, the event includes two keynote speakers and nine seminars guiding female entrepreneurs on vital and current topics.

Ratliff answers questions about the event and tips for catering to a female audience:

What unique challenges do women entrepreneurs face that are addressed at this event?

"This conference has a succinct theme: no theory, philosophy or fluff, just an arsenal of ideas and practical ammunition to help battle women's most difficult business challenges. This educational conference tackles the issues that affect profits and productivity. With that said, our focus is to provide practical, relevant tips, tools and strategies these business owners can immediately implement the very next day. We address the basic profit-generating topics like sales, marketing, publicity, advertising, business planning and finances. Attendees leave with an immense amount of value for the $89 entry fee."

What are your top tips for catering to a female crowd at an event such as this?

"Our format is unique in several ways. We only showcase women speakers, most of whom are local, successful business owners. This way the attendees can actually visit them at their place of business after the event. We offer an expo element to the conference including 45 to 50 exhibits that showcase business resources to the attendees.

Additionally, we offer a retail row of products and services that women love such as clothing, jewelry, makeup and more. I invented a networking kiosk that stands in the foyer

Content not available in this edition

of the exhibit area and has room for 300 business cards. Attendees put a stack of cards in a slot and take whatever other cards interest them — offering a great networking opportunity. We host an after party called the Meet the Speakers Reception where the women can get up close and personal to the speakers at a cocktail party. Instead of a simple program, we provide a program binder that has all the speakers handouts inside, along with speaker biographies, sponsor ads etc. The binder allows the participants a way to get everyone's information even if they cannot attend each session."

Sources: Debbie Drotar, Greater Phoenix Chamber of Commerce, Phoenix, AZ. E-mail: ddrotar@phoenixchamber.com. Susan Ratliff, Susan Ratliff Presents LLC, Phoenix, AZ. E-mail: Susan@susanratliff.com

Expand Partnerships With a Community Internship Program

When officials at the Columbus Chamber of Commerce (Columbus, OH) asked members about workforce issues, finding skilled entry-level talent emerged as a major challenge.

"Large corporations recruit at universities across the country, but small- and medium-sized businesses don't have those kinds of resources. They need help," says Andrea Applegate, director of workforce development.

To provide such assistance, chamber officials launched a program, based around the Web portal www.ColumbusInternships.com, that matches college students with regional employers offering internships.

Because students apply directly to employers, chamber efforts focus primarily on promoting the program and helping employers create outstanding internship experiences, says Applegate. Tools offered by the chamber include webinars, video podcasts and success stories, as well as workshops and in-person employer consultations.

Internship services are provided to chamber members and nonmembers alike, most at no charge. "Promoting economic development across the region is part of our core mission, and the internship program furthers that goal," says Applegate. "The program also serves as a member recruitment tool. Employers always have a positive view of internship programs, so businesses that work with us in that capacity are much more open to considering a full chamber membership."

Since its launch in May 2008, ColumbusInternships.com has registered nearly 9,000 students and 800-plus employers. In 2010, the site posted 632 positions, and by year's end, had some 3,400 students using the site.

Source: Andrea Applegate, Director of Workforce Development, Columbus Chamber of Commerce, Columbus, OH. E-mail: Andrea_Applegate@columbus.org

---

Two Steps to a Successful Internship Experience

For internship programs to grow, participating businesses must have a good experience — and that requires planning, says Andrea Applegate, director of workforce development at the Columbus Chamber of Commerce (Columbus, OH).

Applegate says giving attention to the following two areas can pay big dividends in the success of any internship relationship:

1. **Meaningful activities.** "Say your time is worth $100 per hour. Some parts of your job are absolutely critical to the functioning of your organization, but are really only $10-an-hour activities. These kinds of duties are perfect projects for interns — things that must be done, but do not need to be done by leaders themselves."

2. **Extended experiences.** "We urge employers to involve interns in internal meetings and calls with clients as much as possible. They don't have to be included in everything the business does, but interspersing these kinds of experiences gives them a more rounded base for future employment and creates a more enjoyable and productive experience for everyone."

Quickly Assess Internship Positions

Programs connecting college students with businesses that offer internships can benefit both communities and chambers of commerce, but care must be taken to prevent such programs from monopolizing chamber resources.

Andrea Applegate, director of workforce development at the Columbus Chamber of Commerce (Columbus, OH) and administrator for www.ColumbusInternships.com, discusses steps to evaluate employers and potential internships quickly and efficiently.

- **Initial review.** Applegate begins by ensuring that all employers meet general program requirements, including geographic location within the immediate Columbus region.

- **Internet research.** If an employer is questionable, Applegate does a quick Google search to learn more about the organization and its history in the community.

- **Further development.** If a proposal is not fully developed or Applegate is still unsure about the employer, she will direct officials to resources on the chamber website, send dates of internship development workshops and ask the business to submit a revised proposal.

- **Redirection.** It sometimes becomes clear that an employer is offering part-time jobs rather than true internship positions. In these cases, Applegate directs the organization to online job boards.

Increase Labor Force With Membership Interns

With 12 college students working alongside them, staff at the Kalamazoo Regional Chamber of Commerce (Kalamazoo, MI) know a little something about running an internship program.

"Interns give you more manpower. It's as simple as that," says Laura Pecherski, membership sales representative and supervisor of two interns of her own. "We all know that membership organizations are chronically short-staffed in the current economy. An intern program provides extra hands for any project, for little, if any, expense."

Pecherski, a former chamber intern herself, answers questions about practical details of running an internship program.

What kinds of tasks can membership interns do?

"We have positions in two areas: membership sales and membership administration. Sales interns do a lot of lead generation. They compile lists of businesses that are not in our database and have never been approached. Sometimes they also do appointment-setting and accompany us on sales meetings. The administration interns do anything that helps staff members focus on selling memberships — managing schedules, processing paperwork, preparing materials for appointments."

Who are your interns and how do you recruit them?

"Our interns are all students from area colleges and universities. We stay in contact with the career services department of each, and send them positions to post on their internship/career opportunities pages."

How do you interview prospective interns? What do you look for?

"I begin by reviewing resumes, because they give such a good idea of how professionally candidates can present themselves. Mistakes and misspellings usually weed out about half of the candidates. The rest (about six to ten, usually) I interview by phone to see whose interests most match the work we do."

What is an appropriate time frame for an internship?

"We have done one-semester internships, but two semesters, 12 to 15 hours a week, is better. The longer interns are with us, the more familiar they become with our work and the more effective they can be."

Should interns be paid?

"Some of our internships have a small stipend and some are unpaid. Each department has a small monthly budget for paid interns and those in the membership department can also earn a commission on memberships they sell."

If an organization wanted to start an internship program, what should they be sure to do?

"Just like new employees, new interns reduce productivity before they raise it, so you want to train them as quickly as possible. To do this, we have an intern orientation at the start of each semester. We give them an intern handbook and clearly lay out what will be expected of them. Getting all the rules and policies out in the open saves us time in the long run, and the interns appreciate it because they don't have to wonder about this or that question."

Source: Laura Pecherski, Membership Sales Representative, Kalamazoo Regional Chamber of Commerce, Kalamazoo, MI.
E-mail: lpecherski@kazoochamber.com

Content not available in this edition